TIME

VISIONS
of
HEAVEN

A Journey Through the Afterlife

PERCHANCE TO DREAM *Genesis contains the story of the Hebrew patriarch Jacob, who while sleeping is awed by a vision of a ladder stretching above to the glorious house of God in the sky.*

CONTENTS

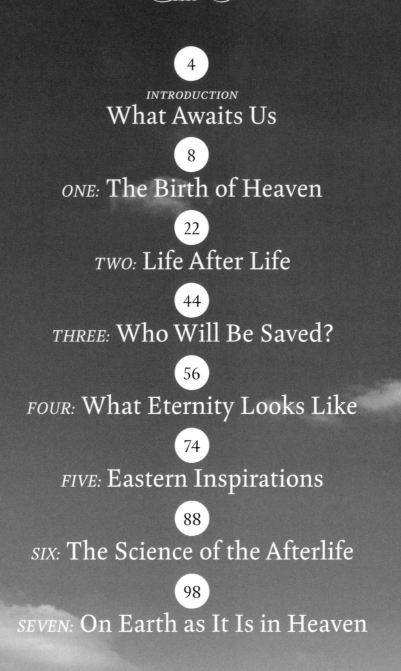

Lisa Miller is a contributing editor at *New York* magazine. Author of *Heaven: Our Enduring Fascination with the Afterlife*, she has written extensively about American religion, faith and spirituality for the *Wall Street Journal*, the *Washington Post* and *Newsweek*. She lives in Brooklyn with her husband and daughter.

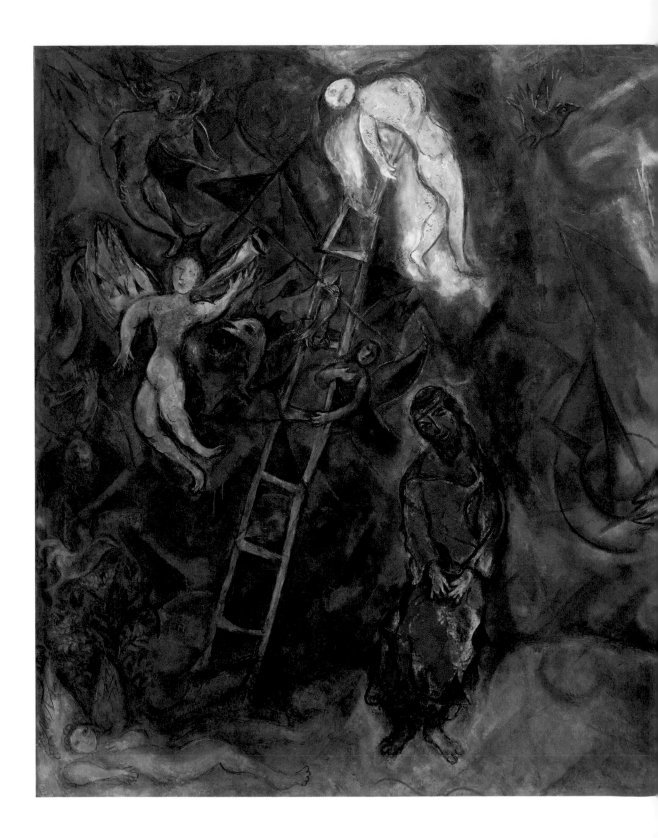

what awaits us

JACOB'S DREAM
The Hebrew patriarch's vision of a ladder ascending to heaven is vividly depicted by painter Marc Chagall.

He was a newcomer to the clan, an orphan with the African name Lipopo

—and he died, unexpectedly, of pneumonia. It was a shock to the whole extended family, and though none of those who were present at the time of his death knew Lipopo very well, they tenderly cared for him, keeping vigil over his corpse and grooming it carefully, as if he had somewhere important to go. And when the caretakers finally came to take the body away, the family matriarch, who was named Mimi, rebelled, protecting the body as if it were her own child. She placed herself between the people and Lipopo, screaming—howling—with rage and grief. At that point, a scientist who happened to be present crumpled with sympathetic anguish. For Mimi was an ape, but her response to the death of a stranger was as human as anything he'd ever seen.

All living creatures die, the first and last fact of life. We begin dying the instant we are born, and humans, who unlike chimpanzees are imbued with self-knowledge, comprehend this terrible reality from a young age. Yet most people, for most of our lives, are able to put it aside. Each of us invents our own story as if we didn't already know the ending: that we will lose the ones we love, that we will expire ourselves. We learn, we hope, we plan, we have children, we work, we keep on trying—and we endeavor to ignore the existential truth, what George Eliot called "that roar which lies on the other side of silence." Heaven, whether you believe in it or not, is the answer to the fundamental howl of human existence: How can this be, that life is a terminal condition? Heaven is the faith that all is not lost. If life has been full of sorrow and pain, then heaven offers respite. And if life has been full of bounty and pleasures, then heaven amplifies those delights beyond imagining.

There are a million disagreements about heaven, starting with the most obvious one: Does it exist? In the Western religious tradition, debates about the nature of heaven have raged for more than 2,000 years. When the Apostle Paul was traveling all over the ancient world preaching the truth of Jesus Christ and the promise of heaven, his pagan audiences laughed at him. A heaven, they thought, filled with resurrected bodies, was the most ridiculous thing they'd ever heard. We are no closer to resolution now than we were then. Is heaven, as Eben Alexander insists in his 2012 book *Proof of Heaven*, "real"? Does it look, as he describes it, "brilliant, vibrant, ecstatic, stunning"? Is God so generous that he, as the Christian pastor Rob Bell argues in his 2011 book *Love Wins*, will allow everybody—including Jews, Muslims and atheists—to be saved? The promise of heaven can be so powerfully motivating that it can compel young men to fly jets into skyscrapers screaming "God is great." It can be so comforting that it inspires conversion from one religious faith to another. The hope of heaven has propelled men and women to build cathedrals with buttresses and steeples, to write poems and songs and symphonies, to paint frescoes on walls and ceilings and piece together murals on chapel floors. The dashed hope caused by catastrophe or grief—*I thought I had this kind of faith, but I just don't*—has been the cause of many a turn toward disbelief.

The trick to having faith in heaven is to do so in spite of the fact that it is, on the face of it, implausible. What evidence in our physical world convinces us of the existence of "another place," where you can live in perfect truth and beauty, forever, with God? None, for even the I-was-there accounts—like those of Dr. Alexander or Colton Burpo, the 4-year-old subject of the book *Heaven Is for Real*, who claimed to have ascended to heaven during an emergency surgery and to have sat on the lap of Jesus himself—are subjective testimony, impossible to corroborate. And heaven-belief becomes more challenging the more you subject it to rational scrutiny. Where is heaven? (In the sky? In every leaf of every tree? Or is it, as Ralph Waldo Emerson wrote, "among us"?) If it's real, then what does it look like? (Times Square, a mountaintop, dinner for 12 at a five-star restaurant?) What do you do there? What happens to your body? (Do you eat, drink, make love?) Are you, in any identifiable way, "you"? These questions are enough to make any person's brain ache, but not enough to push Americans, at least, off course. Eighty-five percent of us say we believe in heaven, according to Gallup, despite a growing disillusionment with organized religion and a growing number of doubters among us. Heaven remains a pillar of even the most liberal liturgies in the Jewish, Christian and Muslim traditions. "Blessed are you, Lord," the religious Jew prays each day, "who revives the dead."

When I published a book in 2010 called *Heaven: Our Enduring Fascination with the Afterlife*, I attempted to guide readers through the biggest questions regarding the idea of heaven in the Western religious tradition. Where is heaven? Who do you see there? Isn't it boring? Why do so few modern conceptions of heaven include an idea of God? The idea was not to answer these questions in any definitive way, but to raise them. For myself, doing that book was a revelation, for it helped me, a temple-going Jew but also a natural-born skeptic, to understand the transforming power of faith in a supernatural God. The idea of heaven is unbelievable, yet to believe in it is one of the most powerful sources of comfort and hope a human being might have.

The desire to defy death is so primitive that even before they believed in a heaven as we understand it today, populated with the souls of loving, departed grandparents and crisscrossed with streets of gold, proto-humans believed in something like an afterlife. Even prehuman creatures, in other words, believed in something beyond the end. We know this because they were buried with things—and why else would a community or a family put a loved one to rest with bones and tools and small, edible seeds unless those things were thought to be either precious or useful to them wherever they were going? In a cave in the mountains of northern Iraq, archaeologists in the 1960s discovered a Neanderthal burial site from about 50,000 years ago. There, a woman seems to have been interred on a bed of boughs and flowers, leading scientists to guess at a religious rite devoted to her continued comfort and care. In 1999 the skeleton of a boy thought to have been buried 25,000 years ago was discovered in a cave in Portugal. He was buried with deer and rabbit bones and a pierced periwinkle-shell ornament in a grave in which pine branches had been burned. His body was covered with red ocher pigment. "He was probably quite important to his people, and was accorded special attention in death," according to the journal *British Archaeology*.

Consider this book, then, a brief tour of the idea of heaven, mainly in the West, starting with its conception in the pre-Christian Jewish world, moving through its development as Christianity matured, and into the Middle Ages as Islam was born. I begin by outlining centuries of celestial questions and themes, designed to prod a reader to consider what he or she believes, to hold up one mirror and then another to the images of heaven that reverberate down the ages: What does Scripture say about life everlasting? What does tradition say? How do real people express their belief and how does that compare with what religious authorities teach? I then go on to discuss the problem of heaven being used as a radically intolerant idea: How does a heaven that consoles so many prompt others to murder? Later chapters describe heaven's cultural legacy, explore the influence of Eastern ideas on Western concepts of the afterlife, and ponder what science might be able to tell us about what awaits us after we die.

It is my firm conviction that many of us who say we believe in heaven have not sufficiently wrestled with the puzzles and perplexities wrapped up with the idea. We owe it to ourselves and to the people we love to investigate its mysteries ahead of time, before, like Mimi or Lipopo, we find ourselves faced with the ultimate end and overwhelmed by the fear and grief that accompany it. Even if we can never know the answers, the examined afterlife may influence how we spend our time here on earth.

1

the birth of heaven

A third-century Roman
fresco portrays children
picking roses in Elysium,
the ancient Greek notion
of paradise.

Until about 200 B.C., most people did not believe in heaven. People believed in afterlives and underworlds, of course. The Greeks believed their heroes went to the Elysian Fields, and the Egyptians thought their pharaohs ascended to the sky, where they lived as gods.

But heaven as we think of it today—the home of God, a perfect place, populated with loved ones and angels, where all souls may go after death if they live the right kind of life (with "right" being open to wide interpretation)—was not a place, or an idea, that people conceived of.

In the land that we now call Israel, a conceptual big bang occurred in the centuries before the birth of Jesus, and this explosion changed forever the way people thought about life after death. Like all major shifts in human understanding, this one seems in retrospect to have been inevitable, but at the same time its origins are utterly mysterious and complex.

The tribe of people who would eventually come to be called Jews lived in a verdant land that they called Canaan. They were different from their neighbors, the Canaanites, because they believed in one God, while the Canaanites had many. These people, whom Scripture calls the Hebrews, did not initially have anything like heaven. But they did have an afterlife, and it resembled in many ways the one the Canaanites believed in.

The Hebrews of 1500 to 2000 B.C. buried their dead in caves, and within the caves they placed things—oils and other liquids, food, weapons, jewelry—they thought their loved ones might need in the afterlife. They believed, further, that unless they placated their dead with frequent gifts, and possibly rituals, parties and prayers, the dead would rise to haunt them; they would ruin their crops and visit diseases upon their children.

BOOK OF THE DEAD
In an Egyptian funerary text dating to the period of 1069–945 B.C., the deceased meets the falcon-headed god Horus and Hathor, goddess of love. These documents were placed in tombs to help the dead navigate the afterlife.

SACRED SITE
The Tomb of the Patriarchs in the West Bank city of Hebron is the supposed burial place of Abraham, Isaac and Jacob.

The Hebrews of that time lived in multigenerational family clusters, in small houses atop their family burial caves. The house, and the cave beneath it, defined the Hebrews' world. A mature couple of childbearing age would sleep in a master bedroom; grandparents would sleep in the chamber next door. And when the grandparents died, they would simply be rotated to another space, beneath the house, where the bones of their ancestors already lay, sometimes generations of them, lining the perimeter of the tomb. The dead, who were thought to exist somewhere in another realm, could be restless and troublesome at times, and the job of the living was to placate them into some kind of docility. "You've got to take care of the dead," the archaeologist Rachel Hallote, who teaches on the Purchase campus of the State University of New York, once told me, "because if you don't, they might wreak havoc on your life."

Scholars call this practice among the tribal Hebrews "the Cult of the Dead," and they know it existed because, along with the archaeological evidence, the Torah warns against the practice. (A good rule of thumb when reading Scripture: if the Bible exhorts readers not to do something, you can be pretty sure that people around the time of the writing were doing it.) "No one shall be found among you ... who practices divination, or is a soothsayer, or an augur, or a sorcerer, or one who casts spells, or who consults ghosts or spirits, or who seeks oracles from the days," reads a verse in Deuteronomy. Anyone who raises the dead shall be cut off from God, Leviticus promises, and "stoned with stones."

The authors of the Torah were monotheists in a pagan world. They insisted on one God, while their neighbors believed in many; theirs was a minority view. They condemned the

Hebrews' afterlife cult, because they feared that ancestor worship—the care and feeding of the dead—could lead to idol worship, polytheism and worse. But they did not offer the earliest Hebrews any notion of salvation. The Torah holds no promise of heaven.

The earliest Jews never imagined that they or their loved ones would go to any place like heaven. The best they could hope for, after death, was a long and peaceful sleep and the prosperity and respectability of the generations that succeeded them. The Torah says nothing, for example, about what the patriarch Abraham believed about an afterlife. It says only that his beloved wife Sarah died at the age of 127 and that Abraham buried her in a cave he purchased for 400 shekels. Abraham died, and his boys Ishmael and Isaac, who had been estranged, came together to bury him in the cave where Sarah lay. People today talk about dying a "good death," and Abraham is perhaps the progenitor of this very modern concept, for after he passed he neither appeared to his loved ones in visions nor troubled them with his discontent. He simply died, "in a good old age," as Genesis tells it, "an old man and full of years, and was gathered to his people."

In the Torah, the word for "heaven" is "shamayim," or skies. It means "the home of God," never the residence of righteous human souls after death. The Torah is adamant on this point—God and his angels are the only creatures permitted to enter heaven. From heaven, God rains down floods and fire, he sends messengers to tell the future. The people of the Torah not only did not yearn for heaven for themselves; they feared it. Just before the Lord promises Jacob that he will inherit the land of Israel, Jacob lays his head down on a rock and has a dream in which he sees heaven's gate, an image that terrifies him: angels ascending

RESTING PLACE
A cluster of monuments
marking Hebrew tombs
in the Kidron Valley
dates to Second-Temple
Jerusalem.

and descending a ladder to the sky. Jacob "was afraid," the Bible tells us, "and said 'How awesome is this place! This is none other than the house of God, and this is the gate of heaven!' "

When Jacob dies, he doesn't talk about going to heaven. All he wants is to be buried in his grandfather Abraham's cave. Jacob is living in Egypt at the time of his death, but he explicitly instructs his loved ones to carry his body back to Canaan. "I am about to be gathered to my people," he says, "in the cave in the field at Machpelah ... in the land of Canaan." Jacob wants to be buried in the same cave as his grandfather Abraham; he wants to sleep peacefully there, forever, as his grandfather does.

The Hebrew Bible does offer an alternative to the long and restful silence that it bestows upon Abraham and Jacob and its most righteous patriarchs. This is Sheol, a shadowy underworld where restless souls wander. Sheol is the destination for people whose lives were unfulfilled, who displeased God, or failed to have children, or died too young. In Sheol, souls exist entirely disconnected from God. No one wants to go there, and from Sheol no one returns. Job mourns:

> As the cloud fades and vanishes,
> So those who go down to Sheol do not come up;
> They return no more to their houses,
> Nor do their places know them anymore.

Looking back carefully through history and Scripture, one finds that the Torah's blanket refusal to admit human souls to heaven is perhaps not so blanket after all. The book of Genesis talks about a man named Enoch, mentioned first in a long list of "begats." Enoch seems unremarkable except for this: the Bible gives him an extraordinary destiny. "And Enoch walked with God; then he was no more for God took him." His existence changes in an instant; no longer is he walking upon the earth. He exists with God, in the sky. The Bible does not say what Enoch might have done to deserve this fate; it does not even say that Enoch dies. But the idea that certain special people might, in certain special circumstances, go to shamayim to be with the Lord was at least a possibility. The other exceptional case is Elijah, the prophet for whom Jews open the door during their Passover seders. Elijah is just walking along with his disciple Elisha when he is "taken up." "A chariot of fire and horses of fire" appears, "and Elijah ascended in a whirlwind into heaven." The Torah says that humans don't go to heaven, in other words, except in the rare, extraordinary cases when they do.

There are reasons that by the fifth century B.C., the Jews may have begun to think about something like heaven. In 586 B.C., the Babylonian king Nebuchadnezzar sacked the Temple in Jerusalem, the most sacred place in Judaism, the center of all Jewish religious, commercial and social life, and drove the Jews out of their city and to the place the psalmist calls Babylon, which is modern-day Iraq. There is no good record of how the Jews lived in their exile, but the evidence that does exist suggests that they were relatively comfortable. Fifty or so years into their Babylonian tenure, the Jews were able to live as citizens of the great Persian Empire, of which Babylon was part, a region that extended west to modern-day Turkey and east to what is now India. They contributed taxes and troops when required, and in exchange they absorbed some of the empire's highest values: tolerance, literacy, freedom of religion. It was the Jews' first experience of being a distinct group, far from home, their coherence enhanced and even aided by their idiosyncratic monotheism. In Babylon, they

THE GREAT BEYOND
A 17th-century Russian painting portrays the prophet Elijah ascending in a horse-drawn chariot of fire, leaving behind his disciple Elisha on earth. In the Torah, only rare, extraordinary humans go to heaven.

were allowed to pray and worship as they had back in the land that we now call Israel.

But they were not insulated. In the way that people do, they also absorbed some of the tenets of a faddish and growing Babylonian religion called Zoroastrianism. The religion had originated about a thousand years earlier in central Asia, in the mountains of modern-day northern Pakistan and Afghanistan and was rooted in the teachings of a prophet named Zoroaster, or Zarathustra. This prophet had a number of ideas that closely resemble the Western heaven. He taught about a judgment after death at which an individual who had been good in life might safely cross a razor-thin bridge into a kind of paradise sometimes called the House of Song, whereas those who had been bad would fall off the bridge into a stinking pit. He also taught about a cataclysm, the culmination of an otherworldly battle between the armies of light and the armies of darkness. At this apocalypse, a series of Saviors would appear, and the earth would be perfected. The dead would rise and, together with their souls, would enter a brand-new paradise. The Zoroastrians had two main gods, not one, and as strict monotheists, the early authors of the Jewish religion officially disapproved. Yet many of these ideas seeped into the Jewish mind and became embedded in the religion—the same religion that would eventually give birth to Christianity.

The Jews' interest in worldliness, in assimilation, in collecting and absorbing ideas from the broader culture, only increased when, around the year 200 B.C., they started to flock back to Jerusalem, now in the Hellenistic period. "There is no question, hands down," the late Bible scholar Alan Segal once told me, "that the Greeks were the most important influence on what we think about heaven." Thanks to the Greeks, the Jews began to think of their souls

ANCIENT HEROES
A woman pauses outside a fire temple in present-day Mumbai after praying on Navroze, the Indian Zoroastrian New Year. The Persian prophet Zoroaster's ideas about the afterlife resemble Western notions of heaven.

IMMORTAL SOUL
*Condemned to death
for disrespecting the
gods, Socrates, in his
final moments, offers a
dramatic notion of the
afterlife as an existence
in an invisible realm
with the departed.*

as distinct from their bodies, able to ascend to God on their own. Already Jews believed in something they called *neshamah*, or spirit, the breath of God that animated each person. "And the Lord God," Genesis says, "formed man of the dust of the ground, and breathed into his nostrils the breath of life; and man became a living soul."

But while *neshamah* vivified human flesh, it was not separate from it, and it had no separate destiny after death. The Greeks changed all that, for they believed not just in the concept of the soul, the spark that animated each person and gave it individuality, but in its immortality. This spark resided within the human head and was the source of all the "higher" human desires: the pursuit of knowledge, rational thought, wisdom. The body itself was dirty and corrupt, driving humans to seek pleasure in sex and food, causing them to become ill. The alliance between the body and the soul was thus uncomfortable, and temporary. After death, the soul shed the body like a snake sheds its skin and left it behind to rot; the soul then ascended to the heavens to live with the gods. The height of the soul's rise correlated with the human's success at achieving wisdom in life. In Plato's *Phaedo* dialogue, Socrates says that the soul "departs to the invisible world, to the divine and immortal and rational: arriving there, she lives in bliss and is released from the error and folly of men, their fears and wild passions and all other human ills, and forever dwells ... in company with the gods." The idea, according to Plato, was to make one's baser, physical desires submit to one's intellect, or soul. And then to allow the soul, at death, to be liberated from the body altogether.

In the centuries before Jesus, all these ideas were floating around in the atmosphere of Jerusalem, looking for a home. There was the nearly universal idea that God, or gods, live up in the sky. There was the Canaanite idea that the beloved dead live on, in some way, needing attention, gifts and sustenance. There was the Egyptian idea that kings ascend to the sky after death to live with the gods, and the biblical idea that in special cases, certain people may too. There was the Zoroastrian idea of separate afterworlds for the good and the evil, the final destinations to be determined after the return of saviors to the earth and a last judgment. And, perhaps most important, Greeks had the idea of an eternal soul that ascends to live with God under the right circumstances. The Jews were already displaying a readiness to see themselves and their ultimate destinies apart from the bones that lay beneath the ground, but they would need a cultural revolution to fuse it all together.

Some of the inhabitants of Jerusalem had never left the hilltop on which the city sits, where they lived in small, cramped houses that afforded them a view of their wrecked Temple. These were the poorer Jews, so far beneath Nebuchadnezzar's notice that he never bothered to banish them to Babylon. And so they had existed for centuries, scraping by, holding on tight to their monotheism, nursing the wounds and the insults inflicted upon them by their conquerors. They were not inspired by or drawn to Greek ideas about the world. They had not encountered Zoroastrian concepts of something like heaven and something like hell. When the rich Jews of the diaspora began to reenter Jerusalem carrying with them fancy goods made of gold, silver and leather, and when they began to seize power, rebuild the Temple and use its storehouses as caches for their high-end possessions, they drew the antipathy of the lower-caste Jews, who had been suffering in relative silence for nearly 400 years.

In the year 175 B.C., under the rule of a Syrian king named Antiochus IV, there erupted among the Jews in Jerusalem a series of skirmishes, between rich and poor, between the assimilationists and the traditionalists, that resulted, finally and unexpectedly, in a theological explosion: an entirely changed view of the afterlife. In 167 B.C., infuriated by the constant fighting, Antiochus sent an occupying army into Jerusalem and forbade the Jews from practicing their religion. He commanded them to eat swine and cease circumcising their sons; he even desecrated the Temple, the holiest place in Judaism. (The outlines of this story are also the familiar story of Chanukah.) A peasant boy named Judas Maccabeus raised a guerrilla army and entered the Holy City. There was blood in the streets, as Jew fought against Jew, and the poor peasant army took on the Hellenistic overlords. Maccabeus won, the story goes. He lit the lamps and rededicated his temple and so saved Judaism for the Jews.

Somewhere on the sidelines, a man sat watching these bloody events unfold. As he watched, he wrote the passages in the book of Daniel that contain the first explicit references in Jewish scripture to anything like what we now know as heaven. Daniel was apparently a teacher and a sage. At first, he advised the Jews to ignore the fighting in the streets, to sit tight and pray to God. But once the streets of his city were full of Antiochus's soldiers, he changed his mind. Perhaps he fled to a cave in the hills, where he wrote the words he hoped would inspire his people to passive resistance. Do not fight, Daniel said. But do not capitulate either. Martyrs, he promised, would be rewarded for their faithfulness in a special way, and the words he wrote would change forever the way people imagined their immortal souls. *Many of those who sleep in the dust of the earth shall awake, some to everlasting life and some to shame, and everlasting contempt. Those who are wise shall shine like the brightness of the sky and those who lead many to righteousness like the stars forever and ever.* With this verse, Daniel gave us heaven.

a brief tour
of the great beyond

Picturing Heaven. Across the ages, artists have reflected—and riffed on—evolving views of the Christian afterlife

c. 1512–1515
Hope, Reaching for Heaven, Stands Among Sad and Happy Men, Joys, and Fear, by an unknown French artist. The personification of hope touches a hand from the sky.

1509–1510
Raphael's Vatican fresco *Disputation over the Most Holy Sacrament* shows the Holy Trinity flanked by the saints and apostles.

c. 1799–1807
William Blake's *Jacob's Ladder* illustrates Genesis 28, in which Jacob saw angels ascend and descend.

c. 1833–1834
Edward Hicks's *The Peaceable Kingdom* refers to Isaiah 11:1–10, in which the lion lives in harmony with the lamb.

1978
In the film *Heaven Can Wait*, starring Warren Beatty, souls wait to board an airplane to their "ultimate destination."

1992–1994
Anselm Kiefer's *Book with Wings*, along with other of the German-born artist's works, is a meditation on heaven's relationship to earth.

2005
On *South Park*, Kenny enters the gates of heaven to help God fight Satan with a video game.

Seven More Heavens. How various religions imagine the place where God resides

Buddhism The Western Paradise
Buddhists of the Pure Land schools can achieve rebirth in wonderlands that are way stations toward Nirvana—the ultimate cessation of ego and desire. For example, the Buddha Amitabha has vowed that all who meditate and call on his name can enter his Pure Land, the Western Paradise, to be brought along to full enlightenment.

Tibetan Buddhism Mount Kailasa
No human being has ascended Mount Kailasa in the Himalayas, but pilgrims of many faiths circumambulate it. Tibetan Buddhists associate it with Demchog, the central deity of an archetypal mandala. Kailasa is also the residence of the great Hindu god Shiva, whose meditative power emanates from the mountain to charge the universe.

Hinduism Vaikuntha
The great Hindu god Vishnu reposes far above the highest heavens in Vaikuntha, a gathering place for those who have achieved *moksha*, or spiritual liberation, through him. It is also called Vishnupada (Vishnu's footstep), and because the god walks the earth, there are terrestrial Vishnupada, gateways to the sacred and eternal.

Islam Al-Jannah
Muslims believe the dead must await the Day of Resurrection to receive judgment. But Islam also provides many details about the rewards and pleasures awaiting the souls who are ushered into heaven (its name means garden in Arabic): rivers of wine and honey and, of course, the privilege of seeing Allah's face.

Zoroastrianism Garo Demana
The religion of Zarathustra inspired many an Abrahamic tenet, including the dichotomy of heaven and hell. After death, souls must try to cross a bridge. The blessed will ease over into Garo Demana, the House of Song. The damned head for Drujo Demana, the House of the Lie.

Judaism Atziluth
While the Torah says little about heaven, the mystical writings on Kabbalah, particularly the works of the disciples of 16th-century rabbi Isaac Luria, divide the cosmos into several spheres and layers, throughout which move the sparks of souls. The highest of these realms is Atziluth, from which the pure deity emanates.

Taoism Da Luo Tian
In ancient China, heaven—*tian*—was not merely sky but a god. Then Confucianism leached the anthropomorphic from the idea. Taoism, however, layered it up like a cosmogonic pagoda. The Jade Emperor governs the universe from Da Luo Tian—the highest of 26 heavens—using an intricate celestial bureaucracy that parallels the earthly administration of imperial China.

(2)

life after life

Renaissance painter
Hieronymus Bosch
imagined humans in an
earthly paradise (near
right) and passage to the
highest part of heaven.

Believing Christians take heaven—and hell—as a matter of faith. They profess its existence when they say the Apostles' Creed, written sometime before the fourth century: "I believe in God the Father Almighty, creator of heaven and earth ... in the resurrection of the body and the life everlasting."

They affirm it when they recite the Lord's Prayer: "Thy kingdom come, thy will be done," believers chant, "on earth as it is in heaven." But precisely what this "heaven" is—or what it means—has been the subject of centuries of debate. As a Jew, Jesus would have inherited the legacy of Daniel and believed in something like heaven, a permanent home with God after death as a reward for righteous behavior in life. But what he actually said about it, taken as a whole, creates a crazy-quilt picture of the afterlife.

In the Gospel of Matthew, Jesus talks about heaven in metaphors. It is a field that the farmer sows. Its properties are as mysterious as a mustard seed or the yeast in dough. It is as wide as a fishing net, as bountiful as a wedding banquet. Jesus uses other, more cryptic comparisons as well. Heaven, he says, is like a merchant looking for pearls, a king settling accounts, a landowner who hires men for his vineyard. With these parables, Jesus seems to be saying that heaven is a place both known and unknown, like this world but unlike it—a place of love and justice, big enough to accommodate all the souls in the world, but open only to some. He is unmistakable on the question of the poor: it is easier for them to gain heaven than the rich, he says, who will find it harder to get in than a camel trying to fit through the eye of a needle. He advises followers not to hoard wealth on earth. "Store up for yourselves treasures in heaven," he says, "where neither moth

READY FOR THE RISING
Christians pray on Holy Thursday, the feast day commemorating the Last Supper before Christ's death, at St. Thomas Chaldean Church in Sarcelles, France.

nor rust consumes." He adds that to inherit heaven, people must become innocent, like little children. Righteous acts were important to Jesus—he was a Jew, after all, and had inherited a code of law that applied to every aspect of life—but humility was too.

But on all the bigger questions, Jesus was silent or, worse, cryptic. And neither the Jewish tradition that precedes Christianity nor the Muslim one that follows it contributes much additional clarity. The history of heaven in the West, then, is a series of disputes going down through the millennia, debates around a few crucial questions about which priests and theologians and philosophers and the faithful have long furiously disagreed. Less than 50 years after the death of Jesus, people were already taking sides:

Where is heaven? Is it an entirely different realm, occurring out of regular time, as the apostle Paul suggested, or is it here on earth, among the believers, or inside each and every one of us?

What does heaven look like? A city? A garden? A banquet? A stadium in the form of a celestial rose, as Dante envisioned in his *Paradiso*?

When do you go to heaven? When you die or at the end of the world or, somehow, both?

What happens to your body in heaven? Do you bring it with you, so that you are recognizably you, doing all the things that bodies usually do? Or do you leave it behind, as the Greeks supposed, and ascend to the sky as a spark, a spirit, an ephemeral soul?

Who do you see in heaven? The saints? The Blessed Virgin? The biblical patriarchs? Your grandmother? Your football coach? Your long-deceased favorite pup? Or is heaven unpeopled—a bright, ecstatic communion with God—and if you imagine it this way, do you include a soundtrack (Bach, Mozart, Michael Jackson, Carrie Underwood)?

Perhaps the most vexing question of all is this one: Are the centuries of stories and songs, paintings and poems about heaven merely metaphors for a place or a state of being impossible to describe in human language? Or are they real portraits of a real place that exists beyond earth, accessible if only we had extraterrestrial Google maps and a divinely directed Siri to lead us there? Here, then, a brief tour through some of these debates as they've unfolded through the ages.

WHERE IS HEAVEN? The Jews, as we've seen, thought God lived in the sky, for the sky was the source of life-giving rain and sunshine, as well as storms and drought that might afflict generations. Again, the Hebrew word for heaven, shamayim, is also the word for "skies." When Daniel gave heaven to the Jews two centuries before Jesus, he imputed to them an eternal destiny, in the sky, where they would be "like the stars, forever and ever." As the world expanded, through exploration and, later, science, ideas of heaven's geographical location shifted dramatically.

Medieval Muslims, Jews and Christians all imagined heaven as a realm both in the sky and beyond it, which might be attained by ascending through various levels, rings or spheres of ever-increasing beauty and goodness until, at last, one reached the home of God. This home was often called the Empyrean Heaven, the highest realm, a roof overarching all the other tiers, made of fire and light. In Muslim tradition, the prophet Muhammad goes on a "Night Journey." After rising through seven spheres to heaven, he finally meets Allah, who tells him that Muslims must pray 50 times a day. (On his descent, he bumps into Moses, who says that 50 is an unattainable number, and Muhammad returns to Allah to bargain him down to five.)

NIGHT JOURNEY
A 16th-century Persian miniature, made to illustrate the work of the poet Nizami Ganjavi, depicts the Miraj, the dramatic, angel-flanked ascension of a veiled Muhammad into paradise on horseback.

As nations' conquering impulses were rewarded with the discovery of new lands, heaven began to appear on maps. Christian monks in the Middle Ages believed that the Garden of Eden existed somewhere on earth, and through or beyond Eden was heaven. In an effort to orient Christian believers properly in the world, these monks drew maps, less for navigational purposes than to illustrate the primacy in the world of Christ and heaven. Eden was often in the East—on the Ebstorf map, created in the 13th century, it is beyond China and behind a ring of mountains. On the Hereford map, created in 1300, Eden sits behind a high, impassable wall. Heaven exists, these maps seems to say, but you can't get there from here.

For my research, I spoke to the Harvard University astrophysicist Owen Gingerich about the location of heaven. He is a Christian believer and also someone who has spent his life looking at the great beyond through a telescope. Copernicus, who discovered that the planets revolve around the sun and that outer space is essentially boundless, dramatically changed people's idea of the location of heaven. Once they understood that the earth is not a stationary object contained and protected by layers of heaven and ruled overall by God above, they had to reimagine the whole Christian universe. "There was a lot of trauma," Gingerich told me, with "abandoning heaven as a nearby, physical place."

He showed me a drawing from a 16th-century almanac that depicted the sun with the planets circling and stars extending beyond them in all directions to the edges of the page. The joyful angels lived here, the antique illustrator wrote, among the stars, in the "habitacle of the elect." After Copernicus, it was difficult to think of heaven as a blanket covering the world. It, along with God himself, was placed outside the physical universe, in a mysterious Beyond— immense, even infinite, in extent. (Not everyone thinks this way. Some Mormons

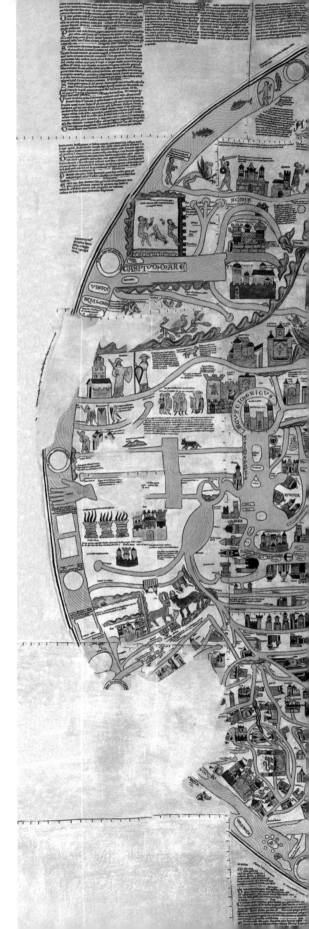

believe that God resides within the universe, on or near a planet called Kolob.)

Gingerich has no problem conceiving of heaven as a place, elsewhere, where earth's natural laws are somehow suspended; he is in the professional habit of such imagining. But a place defined by infinity, perfection and changelessness—that, for him, presents a real problem. For Gingerich, the most difficult question about heaven is not *where* but *how*. How will the human organism, so defined by change, exist in eternity? "Personally," he told me, "I say heaven is a great mystery. If I'm me and I have an infinite amount of time, what will I do to stop from being bored? I imagine I will be learning Arabic and Sanskrit and learning it and forgetting it over and over again."

ANOTHER CONCEPTION OF HEAVEN'S LOCATION—just as compelling as the one in which heaven has a physical location that can be discovered through navigation or space exploration—exists simultaneously with this grand, far-off vision. And that is this: heaven is here among us right now. In the Gospel of Matthew, Jesus says, "The Kingdom is near." Perhaps he meant, as many scholars believe he did, that the end of the world was imminent and that the great reversal of the way things were—the first shall be last, the rich shall be poor, the slaves shall be free—would usher in a perfected new world, a paradise, what the Jews call *olam ha'ba* (the world to come). Or perhaps he meant something else.

After Jesus's death, interpretations of his teachings fell to his followers, but with a logical glitch. If Jesus was the messiah, as his disciples believed, and his death and resurrection failed to usher in the end of the world, then when would this great reversal—the perfection of the corrupted earth that so many apocalyptic believers called "heaven"—occur? Early Christian theologians were forced to think through the problem. Perhaps, they suggested, "The Kingdom is near" meant not an event that would happen soon in real time. Perhaps it meant that, with the arrival of Jesus, heaven existed on earth, in and among the community of believers. Perhaps heaven was not a far-off place or a massive upheaval in real time but something more modest yet no less profound: a thing that occured on earth when people prayed and loved and did good works and strove for justice and beauty and peace. Perhaps heaven was a lot closer than you think.

For support, these Christians looked to the Gospel of John, that most mystical of scriptural accounts: "I have come as light into the world, so that everyone who believes in me should not remain in the darkness." The very existence of Jesus among men and women, this argument went, produced a heaven-like renewal among humankind, no apocalypse needed. In the second century, the Egyptian theologian Origen put forth exactly this idea. He wrote about "the Kingdom" as a metaphor for the pursuit of spiritual perfection. In a meditation on the Lord's prayer, Origen argued that if Christians reject sin and perfect themselves according to God's will, they will find themselves, literally, in heaven. "The Kingdom of God does not come observably," he wrote, "nor shall men say 'Lo it is here,' or 'Lo it is there,' but the Kingdom of God is within us."

This division exists among religious believers still. Among the more conservative faithful, be they Jewish, Muslim or Christian, the idea of heaven as a real place, elsewhere, exists and thrives, as does the certainty of a future perfection preceded by an apocalypse. *Heaven*, the 2004 volume by the evangelical writer Randy Alcorn, is a must-read among conservative Christians everywhere; it describes the actual, physical paradise that will occur after the end: a real place with dimensions and acreage, like this world but better in every way: "Do I seriously believe the new heavens will include new galaxies, planets, moons, white dwarf stars, neutron stars, black holes, and quasars? Yes. The fact that they are part of the first universe and that God called them 'very good,' at least in their original forms, means they will be part of the resurrected universe." Furthermore, he writes, in heaven people will be able to travel to these limitless places and "to inhabit and rule" them for the glory of God.

Among progressives, heaven is more loosely held. It is more comfortable for believers with a skeptical bent to think of heaven as something that happens between people on earth, in their attempts at love or speaking truth or creating beauty or in contemplation of nature's beauty, than it is to imagine another realm, built and populated and as real as this one. On earth, the perfection of heaven, God's home, can be caught in glimpses. This, anyway, is the idea behind Koinonia Farm, a social-justice agricultural community founded in 1942 in rural Georgia and still active today. Having withstood assaults by the Ku Klux Klan for supporting interracial marriage, Koinonia is located on an idyllic grove of pecan trees tended to by peace-loving Baptists and sympathetic believers. "Heaven isn't about going to church for an hour on Sunday, and then way off in the future you go to heaven," explains Koinonia's director, Bren Dubay. "It's about doing what Jesus asks us to do right now." In Marilynne Robinson's 2004 novel *Gilead*, which won the Pulitzer Prize, an aged minister writes a letter to his son with full awareness of his imminent death. He has a friend, he writes, who "says he has more ideas about heaven every day. He said, 'Mainly I just think about the splendors of the world and multiply by two. I'd multiply by ten or twelve if I had the energy. But two is much more than sufficient for my purposes.' So he's just sitting there, multiplying the feel of the wind by two, multiplying the smell of the grass by two." In this view, heaven is not over there, somewhere else, above the stars or beyond the mountains. It's here, right now, in our world and in our relationships, if only we will look for it.

WHAT HAPPENS TO YOUR BODY? Resurrection is, on the face of it, impossible, the stuff of science-fiction horror stories. It means, literally, to rise again, the revivification of dead flesh, yet this Frankenstein scenario is the bedrock of the Christian story, the defining test of faith. Without it, Jesus would have been another Jewish rebel crucified for his insubordination to the Roman regime. With it, of course, he is God, who gives the gift of resurrection to all those who believe in him.

Some Jews of Jesus's time believed in a physical resurrection, and Jesus was most likely one of them. In the Gospels, the Sadducees taunt Jesus about this belief, asking him about a woman who had seven husbands in life: Which was her husband in heaven? (The subtext: If you have a body in heaven, you have sex. And if you have had seven husbands, which one is your sexual partner in heaven?) Jesus becomes irate, accusing them of trivializing: "You know neither the Scriptures nor the power of God," he says. "For when they rise from the dead, they neither marry nor are given in marriage, but are like angels in heaven." People rise with bodies, but not with

the same bodies they had before, he says. His disciples believed something similar. When they rolled the rock away from Jesus's burial cave on the third day and found him gone, their conclusion—that he was resurrected—was foregone.

Pagan skeptics laughed at the idea, which is one reason why the apostle Paul, as he traveled the ancient world, had to mount a vigorous defense. (The Greeks believed, remember, in the foulness of the body and the immortality of the soul; they would not have desired the ultimate reunion of spirit and flesh.) In his letter to the people of Corinth, Paul makes his case with a biting condescension: "Someone will ask, 'How are the dead raised? With what kind of body do they come?' Fool! What you sow does not come to life unless it dies."

The body is like a seed, Paul explains. Its properties in the afterlife will be the same as in life, yet totally different. "What is sown is perishable, what is raised is imperishable. It is sown in dishonor, it is raised in glory. It is sown in weakness, it is raised in power. It is sown a physical body, it is raised a spiritual body." This new body has supernatural powers. The miracle of resurrection conquers—it reverses—death and decay.

Paul's metaphorical explanation, though enduring (and the subject of countless Sunday school lessons), was obviously not entirely convincing. For the church Fathers, the men who in

FINAL JUDGMENT
Flemish painter Rogier van der Weyden depicted a spectacular final scene, with the dead crawling out of their graves to be judged by Christ. The multipanel altarpiece is housed in Beaune, France.

the first several hundred years after the death of Jesus established the tradition of Christian theological reflection, picked up the gauntlet, trying to explain to skeptical listeners how God raised the dead and what kinds of bodies they would have in heaven. They addressed the kinds of questions that must have preoccupied early Christian believers and their pagan neighbors. In the second century, Tertullian wondered what happened if an animal ate a martyr and then a human ate that animal. How would God find and reassemble the human particles? If a person were eaten by a cannibal, how could God separate one human tissue from another?

Augustine, who laid the foundations of Roman Catholic theology in the early fifth century, approached the question of heavenly bodies with all seriousness, designing for his flock a human creature of celestial perfection. In his masterwork, *The City of God*, Augustine suggests that in heaven people will be themselves at around age 30. If they were too fat, they become thin. If too thin, they become heavier. Deformities are taken away, as are body parts that are out of proportion. Women rise as women, men as men. Indeed, in the resurrection women are more beautiful than they are in life, but their beauty elicits no lust. There will be no sex, no eating, no marriage in heaven, as Jesus said specifically. The soul will remember the body's former physical pleasures but without regret or temptation, like a memory of ice cream more delicious than the ice cream itself.

Other Christians preferred the Greek conception. The Greeks believed in a disposable body and an immortal soul, and that idea had found favor with certain Jews in the time of Jesus—those who most wanted to align themselves with the Greeks. And so this concept seeped into the early Christian mind-set, as much as Jesus and Paul preached against it, and took hold there, becoming a constant counterweight to the conventional wisdom. The Second Book of Timothy includes a brief reference to two characters named Hymenaeus and Philetus, who seem to be teaching not resurrection but something like the immortality of the soul. They speak, writes the great Christian scholar N.T. Wright in his book *The Resurrection of the Son of God*, not of "a future bodily hope after death, but purely and simply in terms of a spiritual experience which could be enjoyed during the present life. Certain people had had this experience; they were already, in this new metaphorical sense, 'raised from the dead.'"

Today, Western believers remain split in exactly the same way on the matter of resurrection. Progressives tend to feel most comfortable conceiving of resurrection as a metaphor for something

CITY OF GOD
In a Renaissance-era illustration for Augustine's ancient masterwork, saints are received in heaven above while sinners below either strive for Christian virtue or suffer damnation.

else, meaning, as Wright told *Newsweek* in a 2008 interview, that "Jesus died and was glorified—in other words, he went to heaven, whatever that means." But traditionalists in Judaism, Christianity and Islam think of resurrection as an actual fact, and Wright is among them. The word "resurrection" in Greek, *anástasis*, doesn't mean anything so vague as glorification or spiritual ascension, he points out. "If people [in the first century] had wanted to say he died and went to heaven, they had perfectly good ways of saying that." For Christians, the scriptural basis could not be clearer: the disciples rolled away the rock on the third day, and the body of their teacher was gone. Cleopas and another, unnamed disciple see him walking down the road to Emmaus; in another instance, Jesus joins the 11 apostles for a meal. The resurrection described in the gospels was as real as a stranger who comes to dinner, and the consequence of that supernatural event is that all who believe in Jesus as God receive resurrection—and heaven—as their ultimate gift.

But Christians aren't alone in their commitment to miraculous revivification. The Muslim God is a resurrecting God, and the Quran contains myriad verses describing paradise as a three-dimensional place, populated with resurrected humans who take sensual pleasure in physical things. People wear silk robes and gold bracelets; they recline on couches; they enjoy sex, or something like sex; they drink wine and water; they eat ripe fruits. Residents of heaven speak to each other in Arabic, the language of the Quran, and they always use the greeting "salaam" (peace). Like Paul, the prophet Muhammad faced an audience of doubters and he worked to convince disbelievers of the truth of resurrection. "O mankind," says the Quran, "if you are in doubt about the resurrection / We created you from dust, then from a sperm, then from a blood clot, then from a morsel, formed and unformed, to make it plain to you." Allah, the God of Islam, "is the Truth / It is He Who revives the dead, and has power over all things." He can, the Quran asserts, reassemble bones and reshape fingers. There are modern Muslims who assert that the very physical pleasures of Paradise are metaphorical, poetical descriptions of a mysterious place beyond human imagining, but Muhammad would not likely have been among their number.

Contemporary Jews might be surprised to learn that traditional Judaism insists on resurrection. Since before the birth of Jesus, observant Jews have been chanting a daily prayer called the *Amidah*, which praises a mighty, powerful God "who causes the dead to come to life." Moses Maimonides, the medieval physician and philosopher who established the core beliefs for every Jew, made belief in resurrection the last of his "13 principles of faith"—without a commitment to resurrection, a person could not call himself a Jew. Jon Levenson, an orthodox scholar at Harvard, insists that the Jewish belief in resurrection is based not just on tradition but on the Torah itself—a view that progressive scholars dispute—and he mourns the fact that so many modern Jews have abandoned their belief in favor of something more rational. (In 1824, a group of reform-minded American Jews officially rejected belief in resurrection, saying it was "entirely foreign to our present mental and spiritual state" and they reworded the Amidah to affirm not resurrection but "the immortality of the soul.") Thus, like Paul and Muhammad before him, Levenson is in the position of defending resurrection, to an entrenched culture of skeptics and disbelievers, as a gift to humanity from a supernatural God.

HOW DO YOU GET TO HEAVEN? Over this question, wars have been fought and apostates slaughtered; in confronting it, the faithful find themselves wavering. The question penetrates deep, for it goes to one's essential views about free will and the temperament of God. Are we saved because of the stuff we do? Or are we saved because God loves us?

In the earliest Jewish view, salvation was connected to adherence: the more closely a Jew abided by the many laws that defined his life, and the more devoutly he performed his rituals, the more likely he was to achieve a permanent home with God in the hereafter. Among the Jews who lived in or near Jerusalem, "righteousness"—that virtue that qualified one for heaven—was intimately connected to sacrifice. Many verses in Leviticus are given over to the right and wrong way to slaughter animals, for if properly done, the blood sacrifice of a goat, a lamb, a bird at the Temple's altars would accrue to a Jew favor from God. Out in the desert, the Essenes, an ascetic, communitarian group of Jews who lived during Jesus's time, were also zealous in their adherence to rituals. According to the Dead Sea Scrolls, documents written by the Essenes and discovered in the middle of the 20th century, this community saw the liturgy as an exact replica of activities in heaven. When they prayed, they were not just currying favor with God; they were doing on earth what the angels did in heaven. On the Sabbath, they even denied themselves the daily human habit of defecating; this was not something angels did.

As a Jew, Jesus upheld Jewish law, even if he took issue with specific aspects of it. But salvation, in his view, was not a matter of deeds as much as it was of a faithful disposition. A "righteous" person was humble, childlike. He identified with, and cared for, the poor, the sick and the outcast more than he did with the powerful elites. Most important, a righteous person put God first—before family, social or tribal responsibilities or affiliations. Thus the tension that exists in the salvation debate can be found even in the attitude of Jesus himself: a person destined for heaven must follow the rules of religious law, but at the same time he must submit himself entirely to God. Entirely unanswered by the gospel story is the question prompted by so many contemporary debates, about homosexuality and abortion in particular: What happens when a religion's rules run counter to what you believe God wants?

In any case, the human temptation to ask—and answer—the question "What can I do to gain heaven?" is great, and the Middle Ages were characterized by a zealous desire both to count and catalog sins and to devise church-approved methods of erasing or discounting them. In the fifth and sixth centuries, certain bishops began to publish "pentitentials," handbooks or ledgers of sins and corresponding punishments. These circulated widely, especially in Europe and the British Isles and were meant to help Christians compare one sin with another: Is stealing a loaf of bread better or worse than murdering your mother-in-law or kissing a priest? Incest, sodomy, bestiality and adultery were sins, of course, but so were making amulets, drinking magic potions and eating horse meat.

Having committed one of these sins, one might improve one's chances of achieving heaven by fulfilling the necessary penance. This was often fasting and prayer, but it could also be something more explicitly like torture: sleeping in water or on nettles or nutshells or with a corpse in a grave. As penance, priests sometimes recommended the assumption of "stress" positions, which look like something from the photo gallery at Abu Ghraib: standing upright for hours with one's arms outstretched or bent over with hands reaching toward the sky.

Weighting and ordering sins and penance was an obsession across religions throughout the Middle Ages, and in the 13th century the Christian theologian Thomas Aquinas codified that process of reckoning, dividing sins into mortal ones—which without penance and absolution could separate a believer from God forever—and venal ones, which were less grave. Aquinas's heaven was a stratified place of many levels that correlated to one's degree of sinfulness on earth. The purest souls would get seats in heaven closest to God, and would thus bask more fully in the glow of his love and beauty; the least pure would be farthest away. But because it was heaven, Aquinas stipulated, everyone would be content. "All the blessed see the Highest Truth," he wrote in *Summa Theologica*, "but they do so in various degrees."

UPWARD BOUND
Souls in purgatory are pulled up by the earthly celebration of Christian masses offered for them. Medieval Christians were especially preoccupied with penance and absolution of sins to achieve salvation.

þe saules þat to pgatory wendes
y relesyd þorow help of frendes
... for þai das t þyes
þe holy man saynt austyn says
... sic defu͞otor
... almo͞r posse releuar
... man of helps ar g͞uiall
pgatory auayles þai alle
to say þat in t fastyng
... dede t mes syngyng
man ... þi frendes ar past
... þat hye þe fast
... þou take gode hede
... þe pdon in spede
... synnes þ had done here
... penace not made ye clere
... bil pdon may a man
... þat he may þan
pgatory whyte al ye dett
... may sraswe or lett
... large is holy k͞rk tresor
... is ynogh͞e fore to pay þ fore
... al ye paynys þ det be
ye men of cristia͞nte
... i pgatory auayles
... clerkes yi co͞uns͞ayles
... it spare t kepe holy
... dede in to pur gatory
do here penace whyle we may
... fro pgatory we chyn away
may ye se pdon more worthy is to gesse
is al worldly rychesse

þes saules ar drawue up oute of pgatory by prayer t almes dede

Almos dede

LAST SHALL BE FIRST
Mother Teresa treats the sick in her "Home for Dying Destitutes" in Calcutta in 1989.

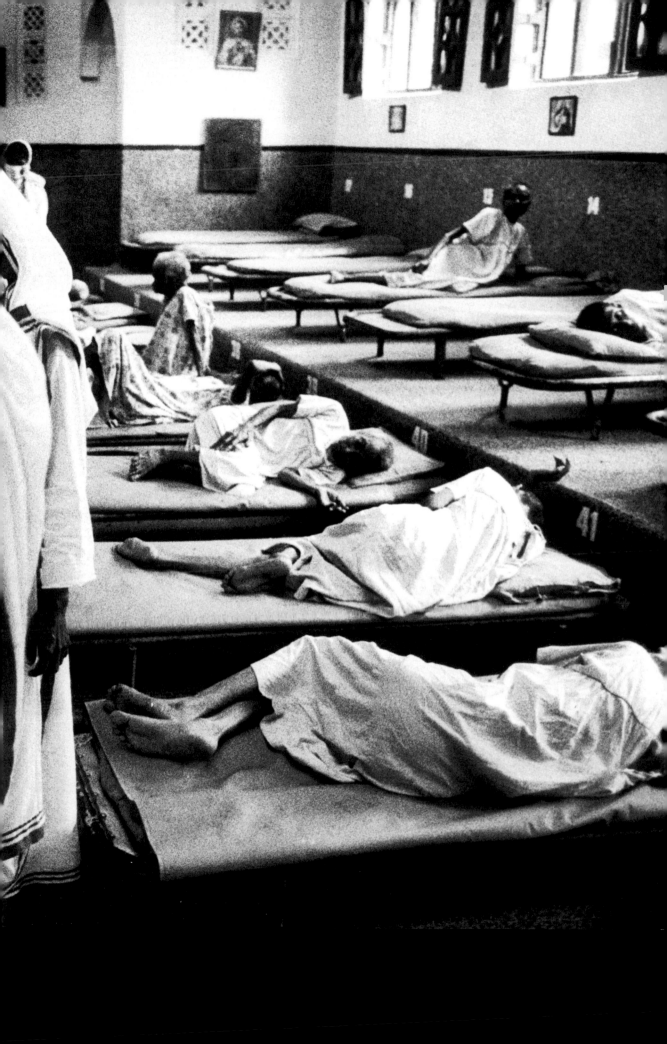

So, the Catholic faithful asked themselves, how might they arrive at the highest possible level of heaven with the least amount of pain? For not only did the church at that time delight in imposing public and devastating penances on the faithful, but it also held out purgatory as a stick, a future punishment that all good Christians hoped to avoid. The only difference between purgatory and hell, it seems, is that the former was temporary. In all other ways, the two states were very much the same. Accounts of trips to purgatory made popular medieval reading; much like the true-crime novels of today, they compelled with their ghoulish accounts of purportedly real events that happened to real people. In the "Legend of the Purgatory of St. Patrick," a knight named Owein travels to purgatory, where he sees humans nailed with flaming pegs to the ground, baked in ovens, turned on spits, dissolved into molten metal and strung up on hooks. These visions, according to the legend, were enough to prompt poor Owein upon his return from the beyond to give himself to Jesus forever. He traveled to Jerusalem and built an abbey there.

By the end of the 11th century, the popes were granting indulgences, official abridgments of future stays in purgatory, in exchange for cash payments. In 1095, Pope Urban II bestowed indulgences on men who went on a Crusade to what is now Turkey, and in 1215 the Fourth Lateran Council promised that crusaders would ascend immediately to heaven without having to stop for a second in purgatory. Cash payments to certain clerics for the recitation of certain prayers after one's death were thought to expedite one's journey to heaven, and because the

SALVATION FOR SALE

During the Reformation, Lutheran artists used broadsheets and pamphlets to mock the Catholic practice of selling indulgences, fees paid to clergy for spiritual favors.

supplications of the poor were thought to be especially pleasing to God, the rich would pay the poor to pray at their funeral masses, giving them candles to hold and shrouds to wear and asking that they encircle their coffins.

Ostentatious abuses such as these helped to provoke the Protestant Reformation. Getting to heaven was not a matter of writing checks and the deployment of power and status to circumvent the agonies of purgatory, raged Martin Luther, a German monk. Luther was reacting to a 1517 campaign launched by Pope Leo X in which indulgences were sold in exchange for contributions to what amounted to a building fund: the pope hoped to raise enough cash to rebuild St. Peter's Basilica in Rome and enlisted the help of a monk named Johann Tetzel to tour Europe, collecting funds. Tetzel had a slogan—"As soon as the gold in the casket rings / The rescued soul to heaven springs!"—that particularly infuriated Luther. One ascended to heaven because of grace, because of the mysterious power of a supernatural God, he said; nothing one did, or did not do, on earth assured one's place in heaven. On Oct. 31, 1517, Luther nailed his 95 theses, complaints against the Roman Catholic hierarchy, to the door of the Castle Church in Wittenburg, Germany, and ushered in a revolution that would divide the Christian West forever. The last related expressly to heaven: The afterlife is not attainable though VIP access, Luther essentially said, and it's not like a baseball stadium, with preferred seating for the mucky-mucks. All Christians have to do is to diligently follow Christ, a saving God. Only then can they "be confident of entering heaven."

who will be saved?

A fresco in the Duomo
in Florence depicts the
blessing and admission
of the faithful through
heaven's gate, guarded
by Saint Peter.

At their best, ideas of heaven comfort and console people and propel them to greatness. Their minds fastened on heaven, people write symphonies and build soaring cathedrals. But at their worst, ideas of heaven have the opposite effect.

They motivate people to murder and they divide people who love each other. Like an exclusive club, an idea of heaven can draw a circle around "the good," separating them from "the wicked," who, once condemned, may begin to seem less than human, less deserving of compassion and empathy and less "like us." Heaven can inflame and justify tribal hatreds, and presumptions about God's ultimate Judgment can excuse bloodshed. In a speech designed to motivate soldiers to slaughter Muslims in the Second Crusade, Bernard of Clairvaux preached on the rewards of heaven for dutiful Christians. "Clothe not yourselves in sackcloth," he said, "but cover yourselves with your impenetrable bucklers ... and conquer a Kingdom which has no end."

Girding soldiers for battle with images of heaven may seem, at first glance, like an antique notion, but consider this: Mohamed Atta did the very same thing before he piloted American Airlines Flight 11 into the World Trade Center on Sept. 11, 2001. "Know that the gardens of paradise are waiting for you in all their glory," Atta wrote in a letter discovered in his rental car, "and the women of Paradise are waiting, calling out, 'Come hither, friend of God.'" This heavenly vision inspired him, he wrote, to want to "strike [the enemy] above the neck."

This is—and remains—the problem with heaven. At a time when more than 40% of Americans marry outside their childhood faith, when about half change their religious affiliation at least once in their lifetime, and when religious doctrine and dogma interest us less than spiritual experience and meaning, the high walls around heaven can appear very forbidding indeed. What young, open-hearted evangelical Christian wants to believe in a heaven that excludes his gay friends? What Jew wants to live in a renewed and perfected world that doesn't hold her beloved, Catholic-raised husband? According to a 2008 Pew poll, 70% of Americans believe

A CALL TO ARMS
Bernard of Clairvaux promotes the Second Crusade in France in 1146, reminding followers of the heavenly rewards awaiting those willing to go to war and kill Muslims in the name of Christianity.

que la terre sainte ⁊ le priu-
ple ⱱpistiens y demourans
peussent secourus et gaudez
contre ses impetueulx assaulx
⁊ leurs tresmautais et auez
remens. et ouuant se tresor
de leglise se donna plain pardon
⁊ remission de paine ⁊ de
coulpe de tous ulces atoue
⁊ a ung chasain de ceubx qui

en faueur et pour aidier la terre sainte prendroient lenseigne
de la sainte Croix ⁊ yroient
en cellui uoyaige. Et combien
que ⱱeist lors et diuerses
parties de ⱱpistiente plusieur
seigneurs ducteurs ⁊ prelatz
Toutesfois seduisit pour
celui temps merualle comme
lestoile iournal au point du

that people of faiths other than their own will go to heaven, and this includes a surprising number of born-again Christians. In a 2006 interview, the evangelist Billy Graham was asked whether heaven would be closed to good Jews, Hindus and Buddhists, and he demurred. "Those are decisions only the Lord will make," Graham answered. "It would be foolish for me to speculate on who will be there and who won't ... I believe the love of God is absolute. He said He gave His son for the whole world, and I think he loves everybody regardless of what label they have."

This Western reluctance to endorse a celestial in-crowd is undergirded by the sense that, around the world, ideas of heaven continue to be used as tools of alienation and enticements to young men to do evil. Guerrillas attacked an upscale mall in Nairobi last year, killing 67 people with guns and grenades; afterward, the terrorist group that took responsibility, an al-Qaeda-linked organization called Al Shabab, released a video called "The Path to Paradise," which hailed some of the terrorists as martyrs. Closer to home, when two ethnically Chechen brothers built and detonated a pressure-cooker bomb that killed three and maimed hundreds in Boston, news reports revealed that the elder brother, Tamerlan, had been watching videos online that advocated jihad, or holy war. "Think not of those killed in the way of Allah as dead. Nay, they are alive, with their Lord, and they have provision," one was captioned. Even in modern times, some regard the slaughter of infidels as a sure path to heaven

It is tempting to accuse Islam of cornering the market on these exclusivist visions, but that would not be fair. In their most conservative versions, Jews, Christians and Muslims all teach that their heaven is reserved for adherents alone. The reason Mormons baptize their dead, dunking children into a fountain as the name of a deceased ancestor is called out, is that without the posthumous rite, Mormons be-

UNIVERSAL LOVE
Theologians differ on who will be admitted to heaven. Preacher Billy Graham has said that God's love is absolute, suggesting that the plan for our afterlife may transcend earthly religious labels.

OF WATER AND THE SPIRIT
To give them access to heaven, Mormons baptize the dead in ceremonies using elaborate temple fonts that rest on the backs of 12 oxen, which represent the 12 tribes of ancient Israel.

lieve, their unbaptized ancestors would be banned from heaven and all its family-centered pleasures. Jehovah's Witnesses believe that at the end of time, only 144,000 souls—the number is from the Book of Revelation—will ascend to heaven to live with God. On the West Bank, ultra-observant Jews see their more secular-minded brethren as walking a pathway straight to hell. "This store burns souls!" yell the orthodox vigilantes who once regularly vandalized a certain electronics shop in Beit Shemesh. Even the peace-loving Jainists consign the spiritually unevolved to ever-colder regions of hell, though as in other Eastern religions, the condemned are given second and third chances to achieve spiritual maturity.

Contemporary American Christianity divides itself, broadly, into two camps around a single theological question: What did Jesus mean when he said, "I am the way, the truth and the life. No one comes to the Father except through me"? Many born-again Christians, who can be of any (or no) denomination, believe that this edict is the defining one. Unless one submits oneself entirely to Jesus in a born-again experience, heaven is unattainable. No matter what other good a person has done in life, without that declaration he is condemned. When Barack Obama met with evangelical leaders in 2008, endeavoring to convince them of his Christian credentials, Billy Graham's son Franklin (who is not as generous a spirit as his father) asked him a pointed question: "Do you believe Jesus Christ is the way to God or merely a way?" Obama knew what the stakes were and answered carefully. "Jesus is the only

DEADLY DEVOTION
Posters hailing the martyrdom of suicide bombers are prevalent throughout the West Bank and Gaza. This one celebrates a Hamas bomber who killed dozens of people at a hotel in Israel during Passover in 2002.

way for me. I'm not in a position to judge other people." (Obama also told me, in an interview at around the same time, that he did not believe that his mother, who was not a Christian, was condemned to hell.)

Others who are not born-again wonder whether perhaps the heavenly gatekeepers are less rigid in their entry requirements, because "righteousness" can be measured in any number of ways. Will a born-again murderer attain heaven and an atheist hospice nurse fail to do so? Do you get to heaven if you go to church but cheat on your wife or lie on your taxes? The question of which deeds, and how many, add up to a ticket to heaven has been a subject for religious authorities for thousands of years. All the while, of course, Martin Luther's concept of "grace" lurks in the not-so-distant background, for heaven is a supernatural thing and access to it, the theologians remind us, is an act of God.

In 2011, a Michigan pastor named Rob Bell, wildly popular among young evangelicals seeking a gentler expression of their faith, published a little book called *Love Wins*. In it, he suggested the impossible to his evangelical fans, most of whom had grown up in churches preaching salvation through Jesus alone. Bell wondered aloud about the existence of hell. If God is love, then why would He damn certain people at the end? Perhaps, he wrote, God has enough love to allow everyone into heaven: gays, Jews, atheists, the unconverted. "A staggering number of people have been taught that a select few Christians will spend forever in a

CONSTANT RENEWAL
United House of Prayer for All People members are baptized by fire hose, a tradition. Most Christians receive the rite only once, but this denomination practices annual rebaptisms.

RETHINKING REDEMPTION
Minister Rob Bell, an avid surfer who finds spirituality in the sport, has spurred controversy by questioning the existence of hell and suggesting that heaven's gates may be open to everyone.

peaceful, joyous place called heaven, while the rest of humanity spends forever in torment and punishment in hell with no chance for anything better," he wrote. "This is misguided and toxic and ultimately subverts the contagious spread of Jesus' message of love, peace, forgiveness, and joy that our world desperately needs to hear." On the night of the publication of his book, Bell participated in a public question-and-answer session at the New York Society for Ethical Culture in New York City. Lines of young Christians wound around the block to get in.

Bell's conservative evangelical peers, however, were not so accepting. Albert Mohler, a leader of the Southern Baptist Convention, called the book "a massive tragedy." So many conservative evangelicals accused Bell of heresy, and so many members of his congregation abandoned his church, either in agreement with the critics or exhausted from having to defend their pastor, that Bell was finally forced to resign his post. In 2013, asked what lesson had taken him longest to learn, Bell told Oprah Winfrey, "There's nothing to prove anymore. All that's left to do is enjoy."

Who's in and who's out continues to cause great pain among believers, between friends and even within families. For my 2010 book, I interviewed a woman named Margaret Toscano, raised in Utah in the Mormon faith by devout Mormon parents. Her church gave her much while she was growing up: a sense of belonging, a sense of specialness, and a connectedness to her family that became her foundation. But as an adult, she became interested in feminism,

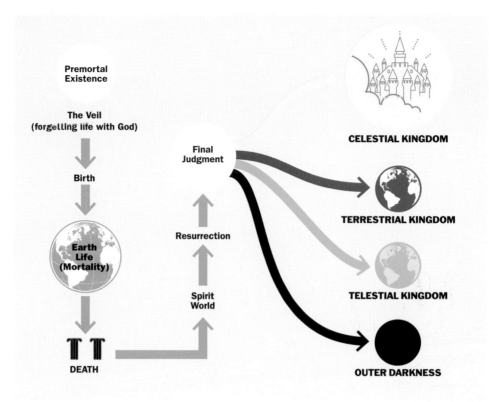

Premortal
Existence

The Veil
(forgetting life with God)

Birth

Earth
Life
(Mortality)

DEATH

Resurrection

Spirit
World

Final
Judgment

CELESTIAL KINGDOM

TERRESTRIAL KINGDOM

TELESTIAL KINGDOM

OUTER DARKNESS

ROAD TO PARADISE
*Members of the
Church of Jesus Christ
of Latter-Day Saints
believe in four possible
destinations after
death, determined by
one's life on earth. The
Celestial Kingdom is
the ultimate goal.*

and as a feminist scholar she wrote papers suggesting that perhaps Joseph Smith, the founding prophet of the LDS church, never intended the priesthood, which governs the church and holds its authority, to be all male.

More than a decade ago, Toscano was called before a disciplinary board and asked to recant or face excommunication. She refused and was excommunicated. She didn't mind this so much, since she had already drifted away from the church and no longer felt bound by its rules. What upset her was that she wouldn't be with those she loves most in heaven.

There are those who say that Mormonism is a universalist religion, in that it teaches that all people will gain life everlasting—that is, will ultimately go to heaven. And this is, in a sense, true. But Mormon heaven is also stratified into levels, and the highest, best level, the Celestial Kingdom, is accessible only to faithful Mormons who follow all its rules. Toscano remains very close to her sisters, some devout and some who like her have fallen away, and she expressed worry to me, in a voice half joking but also full of pain, that her apostasy will separate them in the hereafter. "I don't believe God would separate people who love each other," she told me, but at the same time, she said, she and her sisters talk, in a lighthearted way, about the next life being something like prison. Maybe, Toscano said, laughing, there's a Plexiglas wall between the levels. Maybe there will be a phone that the sisters can pick up, so they can compare their disparate bliss while gazing at one another without touching.

$\left(\ 4\ \right)$

what eternity looks like

In Dante's Paradiso, *the final installment of his three-part* Divine Comedy, *the saintly gather in a celestial rose.*

You ascend to the top floor, your stomach flops; the elevator bell dings. The door slides open, and there it is— the place you've imagined all your life. Heaven.

What, exactly, will you see before your eyes? Will it be, as one friend of mine envisages, a glass-walled penthouse with white shag carpeting that never stains? Will it be an artisanal banquet, tables groaning with fresh fruits and handmade cheeses and, for centerpieces, fountains of water and wine? Or maybe it's an orgy, a dance, a medieval court, a five-star hotel, a high-walled garden, a mountaintop or a beach at sunset. A 19th-century Anglican pastor named Sydney Smith hoped that in heaven he might "eat pâté de foie gras to the sound of trumpets," and around the turn of the past century, American industrialists liked to imagine heaven as a busy railroad station. Images of heaven are as varied as heaven's imaginers. As a general rule, people with terrible lives imagine heaven as the opposite: the first Muslims who eked out their lives in a parched and scorching desert thought of heaven as a verdant and sopping paradise, where cups of libations overflowed and fruits and meats never spoiled. But people who live contentedly and surrounded on all sides by plenty—as many of us do—tend to imagine heaven as resembling their lives on earth, but better: "We are going to sit around the fireplace and have parties, and the angels will wait on us," said the evangelist Billy Graham in 1950, "and we'll drive down the golden streets in a yellow Cadillac convertible."

Despite the historical variation among visions of heaven, certain images recur again and again. The Book of Revelation, written in the last quarter of the first century A.D., is the final book of the Bible. Though nearly 2,000 years old, it remains the source of the most popular and enduring images of heaven. Revelation gives us the "heavenly city," "the New Jerusalem," a bustling place crisscrossed by flowing rivers and streets of gold and encircled by high walls that sparkle with sapphire and onyx. Worthy souls gain entry through gates of pearl. At the center of the city, in a garden, grows the Tree of Life, heavy with fruit. In Revelation you find God sitting on his glittering throne, the white-clad saints singing praises and the angels chanting "Holy, Holy, Holy." A mosaic created in Rome around the year 440, *The Heavenly Jerusalem*, is one of the earliest examples of Christian art, depicting a glittering blue and gold ville with the apostles, rendered as lambs, waiting outside the gates. Revelation is the source material for innumerable hymns and song lyrics ("Oh you can't get to heaven / On roller skates / 'Cause you'd roll right by / Those pearly gates"), almost every joke and *New Yorker* cartoon about heaven—even

GLORIOUS CITY
A mosaic in the Basilica of Santa Maria Maggiore in Rome depicts a triumphal arch leading to a "Heavenly Jerusalem."

the Emerald City, that utopia in Oz.

And in that popular conception, Saint Peter is the gatekeeper, checking folks in or relegating them to an eternal exclusion, like the bouncer at a posh nightclub. This bit of lore has biblical roots as well: In the Gospel of Matthew, Jesus tells Peter that he's in charge of the church going forward. "I will give you the keys of the Kingdom of Heaven." Peter is Jesus's delegate, in other words, entitled in his place to sift the worthy from the damned.

For contemporary Christians, the painter Thomas Kinkade, who died in 2012, offered up images of an unbounded heaven, an untamed, transcendent place, a mountaintop or an oceanscape, a glimmering natural scene. But the walls in Revelation, and in early renderings of heaven, matter more than one might think. Look only at *Christ Enthroned in Majesty*, a fifth-century Roman mosaic in which a gold-haloed Jesus takes center stage but the walls behind him matter nearly as much: high and forbidding, they encircle the saints in an intimate communion with their Lord, while keeping out storms and weather and the unnamed monsters of the sea. In biblical times and for centuries after, a high wall meant safety from animals and enemies and weather. Nothing gave comfort so much as a wall.

And though that sparkling city may provide for us the default vision of the hereafter, the idea of a garden is popular too. Nearly 20% of Americans believe that heaven looks like a garden, according to a 2002 poll. (In fact, the word "paradise" has its roots in the language of the ancient Persian priesthood: *pairidaeza* means "walled garden.") Natural bounty, fertile land, ample water, easy prey, protection from the elements and predators and foes —these were the impossible dreams of most of human history. In the fifth century B.C., the Greek poet Pindar described an island where certain people would go after death: "There flowers of gold shine like flame," he wrote, "some on bright trees on the land, some nourished by the sea." When Muhammad gave Islam to his parched followers, he told them of "gardens beneath which rivers flow" and of fountains "gushing in torrents"; in the medieval Islamic

SAFE HAVEN
A regal, haloed Christ, surrounded by his apostles, is shown seated safely in a brilliant, high-walled throne in the Basilica of Santa Pudenziana in Rome.

SEASON OF ETERNITY
In Italian Renaissance painter Sandro Botticelli's famous Primavera, *housed in Florence, a beautiful woman, perhaps the Blessed Virgin, stands among bountiful fruit trees.*

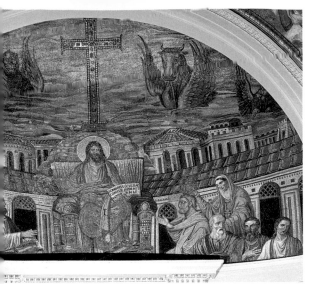

GARDEN OF GOD
Paradise—the word itself derived from an ancient term for a walled garden—is often portrayed as a lush, fertile, peaceful retreat inhabited by blissful saints.

world, prominent men and women were buried in their pleasure gardens, which were shaded, scented, filled with blossoms—an explicit connection between this world and the next. And when Christopher Columbus landed in South America in 1498, he thought he'd found heaven. "I believe," he wrote, "that the earthly Paradise lies here, which no one can enter, except by God's leave."

During the Renaissance, the heavenly garden was a popular subject for painters, for it deemphasized the more stratified, hierarchical vision of the Middle Ages and gave believers a more intimate view. In Sandro Boticelli's *La Primavera*, what some interpreters view as the Blessed Virgin stands in the center of a lush wood on a flower-strewn meadow. Angels dance around her, free of constraining garments, their bodies seemingly weightless. The branches over their heads offer abundant fruit, within easy reach of plucking. In Benozzo Gossoli's 15th-century fresco in Florence's Palazzo Medici Riccardi, paradise looks like Tuscany, with cypress trees in rows, birds flitting among rocky outcroppings, flowering trees and berry bushes in bloom. One of God's angels has wings like a peacock's tail. "Paradise," said the Florentine statesman Lorenzo de' Medici, "means nothing other than a most pleasant garden, abundant with all pleasing and delightful things."

History gives us another vision of heaven, much less pleasing to the enlightened, democratic mind, and that is of a stratified place in which the "best" souls ascend to the very top levels—the skyboxes, if you will—while the least good souls have to take their place somewhere down below. (Medieval theologians get around the fairness problem by arguing that since it's all heaven, everyone is equally content.) This was the popular view in the Middle Ages, at a time when title and rank defined life in medieval courts and when sins and good deeds were being cataloged and weighted on earth with an eye, always, to one's place in heaven.

"True" accounts of journeys to heaven were mass entertainment, the medieval version of reality TV. They circulated around Europe and were translated into many languages. They had a Christian message, but their descriptions of

PARADISE BECKONS
Fra Angelico's 15th-century fresco portrays throngs of joyful, righteous Christians dancing with angels through a beautiful, earthlike garden into a heavenly kingdom, a physical place of light and beauty.

heaven—and hell—were graphic and compelling. *The Vision of Tundale* was one such example, considered in the 12th century to be pleasure reading. In it, the narrator is a knight who has had a stroke and is guided by an angel through layer upon layer of heaven and hell. As Tundale ascends, the righteousness of the creatures he encounters increases.

After a visit to hell, in which Tundale encounters Lucifer himself, a monster with a thousand hands, he and his angel guide begin to climb. First they encounter a place for the "not very evil." Then they pass through a place for "the not very good," where they see "a beautiful field, fragrant, planted with flowers, bright and very pleasant in which there was a multitude of souls that no one was able to count." (There's that garden again.)

In the heaven of the monks and the virtuous, Tundale sees one of my favorite celestial images: a community of tents and pavilions all in gray and purple silk. From inside the tents, he can hear the strains of delicate music: strings and organs, drums and zithers. Above him, hanging from the sky, are gold chains from which dangle goblets, sweet smelling flowers, bells and golden globes. When the angels fly among these celestial wind chimes, "they produced the softest and sweetest song."

The Florentine poet Dante Alighieri took the form of the heavenly journey and elevated it to art. His *Paradiso* gave us an entirely new way to imagine heaven—not city, not garden, but "stadium rose," a place of levels, awash with light, with a living God at the very center. At the beginning of *Paradiso*, light is like air, part of the atmosphere. "It seemed to me," says Dante, who is himself the pilgrim, "that we were in a cloud / shining, dense, solid and unmarred, like a diamond struck by sunlight." As Dante ascends through spheres, he meets saints and martyrs, people he knew in life, and people he knows from history. The light grows brighter and brighter, and finally, when he has reached the highest level, called the Empyrean heaven, Dante addresses the light directly. "I reached the Goodness," he says, "that is infinite."

This is no cartoonish or simple vision. Inside the light, Dante sees that all the variety in the universe is bound together by love, and he understands the wholeness of everything. The light then changes color and becomes three circles—the Father, the Son and the Holy Spirit—and as Dante gazes upon it he sees that it is "painted with our likeness." It is light, it is color, it is three, it is one, and it looks like us. As he struggles to understand the vision before him, he is struck by a bolt of comprehension, and he is changed. He is no longer separate from the universe but one with it. "My will and my desire," he concludes, "were turning with / the love that moves the Sun and all the other stars."

Dante opened the door to countless imaginative renderings of heaven that go far beyond the prescriptions of Revelation or the human yearning for Edenic bounty. Michelangelo, Botticelli, John Milton, James Joyce, William Blake and Seamus Heaney all give credit explicitly to their great Italian forebear.

The Reformation was essentially a purity movement, a move away from the rule-based Roman Catholic Church and also its emphasis on society, hierarchy, adornment and ornamentation. Calvin, especially, discouraged every kind of imaginative rendering; paintings, frescoes, tile work and stained glass were seen as corrupting influences. "Your connection is to be with the Word, the Word over images," the biblical art historian Ena Heller explained to me. "You just need to read the Bible, and you shouldn't imagine it." In Europe, Protestant reformers famously whitewashed the interiors of formerly Catholic churches, to help congregants direct their focus on God alone.

But the reforming emphasis on an abstract communion with God alone in heaven defied every human impulse. Since the species began, human creatures have imagined the afterlife more as a real place than a state of being, where they might see their beloved dead and do the things they loved to do—or that were impossible to achieve—in life.

que bien y entruffent de
front a vne fore dir mille
cheualliers armes tour
a cheual. Celle horrible
beffe auort en fa gueule
deur grime Diablee tree
hideulz et cruelz a veoir

eftorent ace deur Diablee
en la gueule de celle beffe
enfement come deur cou
lombee et faifoient en
Joelle gueule trois portee
Vng merueilleny fen en
grimdeur qui iamaie ne
pouoit eftamdre yffort de

FIERY DESCENT

An illuminated manuscript tells the story of the vision of the knight Tundale, who is guided by an angel through heaven and hell, where he faces terrifying scenes of punishment.

And so a counter-movement began, in which images of heaven became, over the centuries, increasingly "real." In the 18th century, a Swedish mystic named Emanuel Swedenborg wrote about a heaven that was populated and urban and so much like this world that people didn't even realize they had died. In heaven, people became angels, and the angels had homes "like the dwellings on earth which we call homes, except they are more beautiful. They have rooms, suites and bedrooms all in abundance. They have courtyards and are surrounded by gardens, flower beds and lawns." In Swedenborg's heaven, angels lived and worked industriously in communities not of their relatives with other angels who were like-minded; even if they were strangers on earth, they felt that they'd known each other forever. There was romantic love in his heaven, including the pleasures of sex.

Nothing expressed the popular dissatisfaction with Protestant austerity better than the 19th-century American bestseller *The Gates Ajar*, published by Elizabeth Stuart Phelps in 1868, directly after the Civil War. Shattered by grief and by the loss of more than 600,000 husbands, brothers, fathers and sons, American women did not want to hear that the rewards of heaven were ultimate and remote. *The Gates Ajar* gave them an alternative vision, and by the end of the 19th century, it had sold more than 80,000 copies, surpassed only by *Uncle Tom's Cabin* and the Bible.

The Gates Ajar gives us a heroine, Mary, shattered by the death in war of her brother Roy. Her pastor is unhelpful; when she asks him about heaven, he reprimands her for failing

EPIC JOURNEY
A fresco in Florence's Duomo presents an image of the poet Dante holding a copy of his masterwork, surrounded by images of his stratified realms of paradise, purgatory and hell.

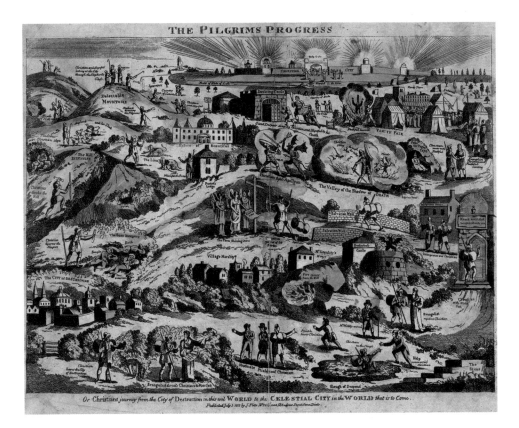

PILGRIM'S PROGRESS
An anonymous map interprets John Bunyan's 1678 allegory, in which a Christian faces various trials on his journey from the "City of Destruction" to the "Celestial City."

to come to church. And so she mourns, alone and depressed, until she receives a visit from an aunt named Winifred, who is recently a widow. Heaven isn't far, Winifred tells Mary, but near. And Roy isn't inaccessible, he's right here. Winifred gives Mary a Christian vision of heaven full of earthly delights and human company. Heaven, she teaches, is full of mountains "as we see them at sunset," trees "as the wind coos through them on a June afternoon" and pretty homes full of flowers and friends. Quoting the British romantic poet Charles Lamb, Winifred tells Mary that in heaven there shall be "summer holidays, and the greenness of fields, and the delicious juices of meats and fish, and society … and candlelight, and fireside conversations, and innocent vanities."

Roy, Winifred tells her niece, is "trying to speak to you through the blessed sunshine and the flowers, trying to help you and sure to love you." When the time comes for Mary finally to join Roy in heaven, she will listen to his jokes, "see the sparkle in his eye, and listen to his laughing voice." She will be able to touch him and kiss him. When Mary hesitantly asks, from time to time, if Winifred's teachings are heresy, Winifred simply laughs.

Today there are no limits to what people imagine as heaven. Transcendent experiences commonly stand in for paradise, as though life in the forever after can be expressed as the ultimate whatever: the ultimate hike or run or spin class (there's a reason they call it "Soul Cycle"); the ultimate cocktail party or family reunion; the ultimate concert or orgasm or restaurant meal. "To me," wrote Ernest Hemingway in a 1925 letter to F. Scott Fitzgerald,

THE KINGDOM AT HAND
Women mourn at General Stonewall Jackson's grave in 1866. Many postwar grievers found relief in Elizabeth Stuart Phelps's novel The Gates Ajar, *which hints that heaven is near.*

"heaven would be a big bull ring with me holding two barrera seats and a trout stream outside that no one else was allowed to fish in and two lovely houses in the town; one where I would have my wife and children and be monogamous and love them truly and well and the other where I would have my nine beautiful mistresses on 9 different floors."

And when there are no rules about what heaven looks like, then an artist can permit him- or herself unlimited imaginary range. Perhaps the most enduring contemporary vision of the afterlife was created by Albert Brooks for his 1991 movie *Defending Your Life*. In it, the hero, Daniel Miller, dies suddenly in midlife and ascends to Judgment City, a celestial way station on the path to his ultimate destination. The movie is, at heart, a love story—boy meets girl and, thanks to her, becomes his better self—but its context is all Brooksian afterlife. Electric trains shuttle souls back and forth between their hotels and the courtrooms in which judgments are rendered. The food in restaurants is always delicious, never caloric, and always arrives before you've finished ordering. Brooks even imagined entertainment for the dead: floor shows, stand-up comedy or, in the Past-Lives Pavilion, a retrospective look at your previous incarnations.

I spoke to Brooks one evening by phone. He is still extremely proud of *Defending Your Life* and admits to getting teary when he catches it on TV. He says he knew it would succeed only if he established every detail of Judgment City beforehand: what everything looked like and how things worked. "It took a lot of thought over a long period of time," he told

JUDGMENT CITY
*Albert Brooks's roman-
tic comedy* Defending
Your Life *tells the
story of a newly dead
man who arrives in
a waiting area filled
with contemporary
earthly comforts.*

me. "I had these charts all over the place, I had to make up all these rules. How long you were there, for instance. You could eat all you want. How does that work? If there was consciousness, what consciousness?"

At the end of our conversation, I asked Brooks what his own personal heaven might be like. He answered in emotional terms. "I don't know," he answered. "It would be great if the movie was right, if someone said, 'You still have a lot of fears, but you figured it out, so come with me.' If I am right, I'd like to be awarded a posthumous Nobel Prize. More than that. Free parking."

Critics of heaven-is-whatever-you-want-it-to-be say it elides the most important thing about heaven: it is where God lives. Heaven is a privilege awarded to the righteous. The reward of living a good life should not be to have all the sex you want with like-minded angels or to eat what you want and not get fat; it should not even be to reunite and make amends with the people you've lost. It should be to revel in a union with God.

This backlash expressed itself most particularly around the book, and then the movie, *The Lovely Bones*. Published in 2002, Alice Sebold's book spent 78 weeks on the *New York Times* bestseller list. Five million copies are in print. The novel is narrated from heaven by a 14-year-old girl named Susie Salmon (raped and monstrously murdered), and the picture it evokes of heaven is as detailed as anything Albert Brooks—or Dante—could have imagined.

TAILOR-MADE ETERNITY

Alice Sebold's bestseller The Lovely Bones, *made into a film in 2009, imagines an afterlife customized with individual pleasures and needs not affected by earthly emotions.*

In *The Lovely Bones*, everyone lives in a personalized heaven, but those heavens overlap. Shot-putters and javelin throwers play in the fields of Susie's heaven, forming a kind of sporty backdrop, but when the sun goes down, the athletes retire to heavens of their own. Susie has a best friend—they eat peppermint ice cream together—but the friend comes and goes, and when she goes, she plays her saxophone in a heavenly jazz band.

The book of Revelation says there will be no tears in heaven, but Susie has not left her emotions behind. She feels vengeful rage at her murderer, as well as typical adolescent alienation. She regrets her inexperience with sex and watches from heaven as the boy she loves gets over her. Christians noticed, rightly, that Sebold's heaven did not corroborate the traditional view. "When there is more talk of heaven in novels, television shows, and pop songs," wrote Mark Ralls, a North Carolina pastor in *The Christian Century*, "Christians must shoulder some of the blame for the fact that visions of life beyond death fail to include God."

But Sebold is no traditionalist. "I've always felt," she told me, "that there were so many rules and exclusions out there in conceptions of redemption and the afterlife—it didn't include me and a lot of my friends. The guiding principle [in my conception of heaven] is that it's inclusive. It allows you to have what you want and what you desire." Sebold may be reflecting the view of a lot of us when she says she wants the high walls around heaven to finally be torn down.

heavenly words

"I'LL SHOW YOU A PLACE HIGH ON A DESERT PLAIN WHERE THE STREETS HAVE NO NAME."

U2

"THAT'S WHAT HEAVEN IS. YOU GET TO MAKE SENSE OF YOUR YESTERDAYS."

MITCH ALBOM, *The Five People You Meet in Heaven*

"We may be surprised at the people we find in heaven. God has a soft spot for sinners. His standards are quite low."

DESMOND TUTU

"As long as the vision of heaven is always changing, the vision of earth will be exactly the same. No ideal will remain long enough to be realized, or even partly realized. The modern young man will never change his environment; for he will always change his mind."

G.K. CHESTERTON, *The Eternal Revolution*

"I never spoke with God, Nor visited in heaven; Yet certain am I of the spot As if the chart were given."

EMILY DICKINSON, "I Never Saw a Moor"

"Earth's crammed with heaven, and every common bush afire with God; But only he who sees, takes off his shoes."

ELIZABETH BARRETT BROWNING, *Aurora Leigh*

"EVERYONE WHO HAS EVER BUILT ANYWHERE A 'NEW HEAVEN' FIRST FOUND THE POWER THERETO IN HIS OWN HELL."

FRIEDRICH NIETZSCHE, *On the Genealogy of Morals*

"HE WILL WIPE EVERY TEAR FROM THEIR EYES. THERE WILL BE NO MORE DEATH OR MOURNING OR CRYING OR PAIN, FOR THE OLD ORDER OF THINGS HAS PASSED AWAY."

REVELATION 21:4

"I DON'T KNOW ANYTHING ABOUT THE AFTERLIFE BECAUSE I HAVEN'T BEEN THERE YET."

MARINA ABRAMOVIĆ

"ASK YOURSELF WHETHER THE DREAM OF HEAVEN AND GREATNESS SHOULD BE LEFT WAITING FOR US IN OUR GRAVES—OR WHETHER IT SHOULD BE OURS HERE AND NOW AND ON THIS EARTH."

AYN RAND, *Atlas Shrugged*

"HEAVEN GOES BY FAVOR. IF IT WENT BY MERIT, YOU WOULD STAY OUT AND YOUR DOG WOULD GO IN."

MARK TWAIN

"Death is no more than passing from one room into another. But there's a difference for me, you know. Because in that other room, I shall be able to see."

HELEN KELLER

"They who believe and do righteous deeds— those are the companions of Paradise; they will abide therein eternally."

QURAN, AL-BAQARAH 2:82

"To enter heaven is to become more human than you ever succeeded in being on earth; to enter hell is to be banished from humanity. What is cast (or casts itself) into hell is not a man: it is 'remains.'"

C.S. LEWIS, *The Problem of Pain*

"In sorrow we must go, but not in despair. Behold! we are not bound for ever to the circles of the world, and beyond them is more than memory. Farewell!"

J.R.R. TOLKIEN, *The Lord of the Rings*

"TO BE IN HELL IS TO DRIFT: TO BE IN HEAVEN IS TO STEER."

GEORGE BERNARD SHAW, *Man and Superman*

"I LOOK UPON DEATH TO BE AS NECESSARY TO OUR CONSTITUTION AS SLEEP. WE SHALL RISE REFRESHED IN THE MORNING."

BENJAMIN FRANKLIN

eastern
inspirations

In an 18th-century Thai wall painting, Buddha, having visited heaven to preach to his mother and other inhabitants, is shown descending back to earth.

Americans love second chances. We extend them to our celebrities, our athletes, our politicians. Robert Downey Jr., once a perpetual resident of Hollywood's rehab centers, turns clean and sober and becomes a top box-office draw.

Jim McGreevey, erstwhile governor of New Jersey (and married father of two), suffers political death after a sex scandal, then comes back to life as a gay Episcopal priest. Bill Clinton, another scandal survivor, has quadruple bypass surgery and rejuvenates, slim and smiling, beloved and beneficent, to represent a nation's conscience abroad and to tirelessly support the political ambitions of his once humiliated wife. Our interest in these makeover subjects goes beyond mere rubbernecking. We hope that in them, and through them, we will find new lives, new roles, new ways to be inspired.

Belief in reincarnation is on the rise in this country, and no wonder. It is the ultimate comeback story, the American dream. Julia Roberts told *Elle* magazine several years ago that she saw herself as a guide or shepherd to her daughter's time-traveling spirit, "someone ... I didn't get the benefit of knowing." One in four Americans claims to believe in reincarnation—astonishing in a country where nearly 80% of people call themselves Christian—and that proportion holds fairly steady among Protestants, Catholics and the unaffiliated (though it is understandably higher among Hindus and Buddhists). The afterlife in Christianity, Judaism and Islam promises an entirely new arrangement—not another version of the same old thing but rather a place, or state, of perpetual perfection. But reincarnation gives believers something that may be even better: a do-over, right here on earth. "Reincarnation," religion scholar Stephen Prothero told me in an interview in the *New York Times*, "means never having to say you're dead."

For many, the belief in reincarnation is part of a much broader interest in Eastern religions, the roots of which can be traced at least as far back as the mid-1960s, when George Harrison took

BORN AGAIN
The Wheel of Transmigratory Existence represents samsara, the Buddhist belief in the cycle of rebirth, wherein beings wander through six realms distinguished by various states of comfort or hunger.

FROM EAST TO WEST
In 1968, the Beatles traveled to Rishikesh, India, to study with Maharishi Mahesh Yogi. The famous trip exposed many Westerners to Eastern religious concepts for the first time.

up the sitar. More than a fad, this exploration of the East has informed and dramatically altered spiritual practice in America. Prestigious universities are setting up entire departments to study the salutary effects of meditation—Brown just started a "contemplative studies" initiative, demonstrating its commitment with 16 devoted faculty members—and estimates have put the number of yoga practitioners at as high as 20 million. This Eastern embrace has occurred in part because it's easy. Eastern religions tend to be less exclusionary than those in the West; Eastern practices and beliefs can thus be incorporated into a Jewish or Christian life without requiring conversion or a wholesale change of allegiance. This kind of spiritual conflation "isn't about orthodoxy," Prothero told me. "It's about whatever works. If going to yoga works, great—and if going to Catholic mass works, great. And if going to Catholic mass plus the yoga plus the Buddhist retreat works, that's great, too." You can be a Jew who practices meditation, a Muslim who vacations at an ashram. A Google search on "yoga in church basements" yields 80 million results. (In its traditional Hindu form, yoga is a way to prepare for the hereafter. The practice allows you to free your mind from attachment, preparing it for escape from not just the human realm but existence itself, which is why in 2010 the theological leader of the Southern Baptist Convention pronounced yoga definitively "not Christian.")

Nevertheless, when your friend says that in a past life she was a Viking princess or an English kitchen maid or an African herbalist or a suffragette, you barely blink an eye. "Past-life regression," the idea that you can uncover your previous lives through hypnosis, has so permeated our cultural consciousness that it's nearly as commonplace as couples

BEYOND A FAD
Thousands gather in Times Square to practice yoga, which has exploded in popularity worldwide. In its original Hindu form, yoga is practiced to prepare for the afterlife.

counseling. Books on past lives—especially *Many Lives, Many Masters,* by the Yale-trained psychiatrist Brian Weiss, but also volumes by Michael Newton and Karen Berg—are massive bestsellers. Turn on Oprah and find her talking cozily with Weiss, explaining how the people you love become angels after they die, how they talk to you and guide your life. Weiss has spent his life defending his theories to his well-credentialed peers: that by unearthing past lives, people can discover the hidden sources of their current pain and thus be quickly healed. At a Weiss seminar I once attended, one man described a previous life in which he managed a large English country estate, reminiscent perhaps of Downton Abbey. Another remembered fighting for his life on a masted naval ship and smelling the acrid scent of cannon fire.

We want to come back to earth to live again, because even the poorest among us regard life on earth as good. Twenty-first century America holds luxuries of which the Bible's figures might only dream: refrigeration, retirement accounts, sex without marriage, storm windows, flush toilets, locks on the doors. Thus reincarnation gives modern Americans the opportunity to enjoy these pleasures again and again and to postpone the inevitable— eternity—for another day. Our infatuation with reincarnation may have Eastern roots, but we have put on it a uniquely American spin. In our optimism, we may be naive, for in the East, reincarnation is no reward but an integral part of a cycle of suffering. You live. You die. You live again. You die again. Nirvana is not a yogurt store or a grunge band. It's not a state of bliss, a beach at sunrise. It's a release from the cycle of pain, an obliteration of identity, a void. "Mere suffering exists, no sufferer is found," reads the Buddhist text. "The

OLD SOUL
The sixth Living Buddha, Dezhub Jamyang Sherab Palden, a young boy chosen in 2010 by top monks, is worshipped at Zagor Monastery in southwestern Tibet.

BREAKING THE CYCLE
Bodies are burned on the banks of the Ganges River in the northern Indian city of Varanasi. In Hindu tradition, being cremated in this holy location liberates souls from the process of reincarnation.

deeds are, but no doer of the deeds is there / Nirvana is, but not the man that enters it / The path is, but no traveler on it is seen."

In Hinduism, the body is disposable; the eternal soul, the *atman* or *jiva*, rotates through this reincarnation cycle, *samsara*, which has no beginning or end. The cycle is affected by karma, a system of cause and effect that we are used to thinking about as rewards, or consequences. Good deeds now will have a salutary bearing on a soul's next life; bad deeds will have the opposite. The goal in Hinduism is to ultimately exit the cycle by achieving *moksha*, release, which accompanies human perfection. Only then do you go live with God.

Buddhism has reincarnation, too. When people die, their souls (according to some strains of Buddhism) are recycled into states (humans, deities, demons, spirits or animals) and exist again, not just here on earth but in different realms, some of which are like heaven and some of which are like hell. In the higher realms, souls experience abundance and ease; in lower ones, they experience disconnection and loss. In the "hungry ghost realm," for example, often depicted in Japanese Buddhist imagery, souls who were greedy in previous lives are afflicted with a continual hunger that can never be sated. In stylized Japanese ink drawings, these hungry ghosts are demonlike, with sunken bodies, often crawling on the floor in search of satiation they will never find.

SHIFTING VIEWS

A funeral home manager demonstrates how a casket is placed in a crematorium. Cremation is swiftly gaining acceptance in the U.S., as attitudes about the need for a body after death evolve.

But while the higher realms may contain heavenlike comforts, they are not, in themselves, heaven. If the whole idea in the East is to escape existence entirely, then even the pleasures of a comfort-laden Buddhist realm work against this ultimate goal, for earthly pleasures seduce a body into wanting to stay and partake of them. Nirvana is the ultimate escape of your perpetual youness. It's exactly the opposite of preserving a unique identity for all eternity; it's a snuffing out of everything, including the soul. "Gone, gone, gone beyond," goes the mantra for the Heart Sutra, "gone altogether beyond, oh, what an awakening, All hail!"

To embrace reincarnation, then, Westerners need to do more than reinterpret Eastern theology to suit their optimistic temperaments. They have to deny doctrines the Jewish, Christian and Muslim religions hold (at least in their conservative versions) as sacrosanct: resurrection and their own traditions' view of the body as sacred. Resurrection doctrine says that an individual is composed equally of body and soul; each is one of God's special creations. In heaven, these two parts will be reunited and a person will live, recognizably, as him- or herself again.

It is for this reason that among conservative adherents, cremation is seen as a desecration of God's work and is thus forbidden. Mormons, Southern Baptists and members of the Eastern

Orthodox Church are particularly adamant that the soul cannot live in heaven without its body. Among modern-orthodox Jews, shivah, the traditional period of mourning, is sometimes denied to those whose remains are cremated.

And yet. Another sign that Americans are increasingly open-minded about the ability of the soul to travel after death without its body is this: the practice of cremation is at an all-time high. Three decades ago, roughly 15% of people chose cremation after death, according to the Cremation Association of North America. By 2025, the industry predicts, that number will jump to more than 55%. This dramatic shift is the result not just of an openness to Eastern ideas about death and afterlife—cremation is a Hindu rite—but to the economic advantages of cremation over burial and to the realities of modern life: with families dispersed as they are, there's no obvious place to put a grave. Even the Roman Catholic Church has recently changed its position on cremation. Funeral masses have always been said over an intact human body, the casket being brought before the altar in a church. But since 1997, acknowledging that economics or family circumstances sometimes make cremation the best or only option, Rome has waived that restriction for Catholics in North America. We are, as I once wrote in *Newsweek*, all Hindus now.

These ideas—that souls have lives of their own, that they move on after the demise of one body to inhabit another—are Eastern, yes, but they also have precedent in the West. Pythagoras may be known by geometry students everywhere for his triangles, but in the sixth century B.C. he hypothesized on many subjects, among them reincarnation, his version of which is known as metempsychosis, a term that is more philosophical, referring to a soul's transmigration. Xenophanes, another philosopher, famously told the tale of Pythagoras's

HUNGRY GHOSTS
A Japanese scroll dating to the 12th century depicts the plight of the gaki, the emaciated, suffering creatures that dwell in one of the six realms of Buddhism. These beings are thought to have been greedy in a prior life.

stopping a man from beating a dog after he recognized the dog's barking as the cries of a friend, presumably reborn as a dog. In his *Republic*, Plato describes a scene of transmigration, a place where souls choose new forms: men become wild animals, animals become men, and the virgin huntress Atalanta morphs into an athlete.

And though conservative Judaism insists on the sanctity of the body and its ultimate resurrection, Judaism's more mystical strains teach something else. In the research for my previous book on heaven, I met a Lubavitch rabbi named Manis Friedman, who had once been Bob Dylan's teacher, and we discussed the rabbi's mystical understanding of the afterlife. He spoke of heaven as a place where souls are active, where they continue to ascend, to learn, to perfect themselves. Souls, he explained, are eternally alive. They cannot die. "What is dead can't live. What's alive can't die. Then what does death mean? This living soul, which cannot die, enters a body, which cannot live. For 80, 90, 120 years, the body lives off the soul. When they separate, the soul continues to live. The soul goes back to the universe of souls. We call it heaven." And then Friedman said this: "When a soul reaches a really high level of closeness to God, it becomes more and more like God and then it wants to come back to earth."

I was dumbstruck. Was he really saying what I thought he was saying? An eternal soul, which exists without the body, travels somewhere after death to join other souls, where they learn to become more like God. Sometimes those souls come back to earth to inhabit new bodies. Was this rabbi, a pillar of Judaism, talking about reincarnation? "Yes," he told me.

At least since the Middle Ages, reincarnation has been a thread in Jewish thought. It is central to Kabbalah mysticism and in the life of any Jew who regards himself as an heir to the mystical tradition. Kabbalah has its roots in ancient oral traditions but became more widely known in the 12th century, when Spanish Jews came to publish tracts outlining the movement's doctrines. The most important of these texts was the Zohar, a series of biblical commentaries attributed to the second-century teacher Simeon bar Yohai. Kabbalistic mystics meditate on the text and on individual letters within the text and, in so doing, produce out-of-body experiences (not unlike the detachment sought in meditation and yoga).

Kabbalists speak of *gilgul*, a revolution of souls, in which souls ascend to God and then back down to earth on a sort of invisible Ferris wheel. Those souls that have attained perfect righteousness remain on high. Those in need of further perfecting, usually by doing more good deeds, return for another try. "As long as a person is unsuccessful in his purpose in this world," reads the Zohar, "the Holy One, blessed be He, uproots him and replants him over and over again." In one popular Hasidic tale, a rabbi is visited by the soul of a dead man who had lived a blameless life until he made one mistake: he boasted of his perfection just before his death. This soul is then reborn as the rabbi's own son, and the rabbi is able to improve the soul through the teaching of Scripture. Once perfected, souls reside in heaven, referred to in Kabbalah as a "reunion with God."

MYSTICAL TRADITION

A man prays in a cave containing the tombs of holy rabbis in the northern Israeli city of Safed, known as a center of Kabbalah. The ancient Jewish practice includes the concept of gilgul, *a cyclical migration of souls.*

When Americans say they love reincarnation and all that goes with it—past lives, second chances, a soul that journeys on its own—they are creating a spiritual system of belief that's entirely new. *Moksha* and nirvana teach us that souls exit this world and cease to exist. Kabbalah teaches that ultimately a soul fuses with God. This is different from the popularly held belief, which seems to be something more like a centuries-long soul-improvement plan. And it's different, too, from atheist belief, which holds that nothing at all happens after death. It's hard to think of this leap into a void as a belief system, since it seems to be more of an absence of one. But even an exit can be a goal.

6

the science of the afterlife

Though our future beyond death remains one of humanity's most fascinating mysteries, research sheds some light.

If you've seen heaven, does that mean it exists? This question is more than a mind-bender. For thousands of years, certain people have claimed to have actually visited the place that, Saint Paul promised, "no eye has seen ... and no human mind has conceived," and their stories very often follow the same narrative arc.

A skeptic, a rogue or an innocent suffers hardship or injury: he is hit on the head, he suffers a stroke, he sustains damage in a car crash or on the operating table. A feeling of disconnection comes over him, a sense of being "outside" himself. Perhaps he encounters an opening: a gate, a door, a tunnel. And then, all at once, he is being guided through other worlds that look and feel to him more "real" than the world in which he once existed. These realms are both familiar and strange, containing music that doesn't sound like music and light brighter than any light, and creatures that may or may not be angels, and the familiar faces of loved ones lost as well as figures from history and sometimes—depending on the narrator—even Jesus himself. The tourist is agape. Words fail. He leaves reluctantly to reoccupy his body and this earth. But the experience changes him forever. Convinced as he is of a wholly different reality, he is calmer, more self-assured, determined to persuade the world of heaven's truth. He tells his story to the masses. "Heaven is real!" he proclaims.

The Book of Enoch, written hundreds of years before the birth of Jesus, tells a version of this story and so does the Book of

BEYOND THE BODY
People who have had near-death experiences often describe an out-of-body sensation. The reasons why have captured the interest of both spiritual and scientific communities.

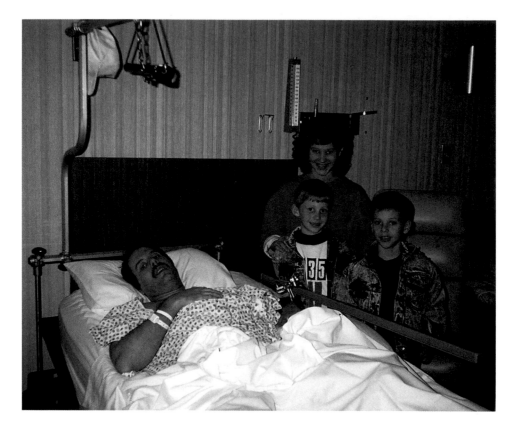

HEAVEN AND BACK
*According to Don Piper,
a Christian minister
who survived a car
accident and had
a near-death
experience,
heaven was "the
greatest family
reunion of all."*

Revelation, Christianity's most foundational description of the sights and sounds of heaven. So do the medieval visionaries whose accounts were to the Middle Ages what reality TV is to the 21st century: "real" events marketed as popular entertainment (with an edifying Christian message thrown in). And despite—or perhaps because of—the increasing rationalism of our times, this narrative genre thrives today. *Ninety Minutes in Heaven* (2004), about a Christian pastor who ascended to God after a car wreck; *Heaven Is for Real* (2010), about a child who sees heaven during surgery; and *Proof of Heaven*, by a Duke-trained neurosurgeon who traveled to heaven in 2012, have all been bestsellers, all following the same storyline. The neurosurgeon, Eben Alexander, said in *Newsweek* in 2012 that his experience convinced him that his consciousness (the soul, or the self) exists somehow separate from or outside the mind and can travel to other dimensions on its own. "This world of consciousness beyond the body," he wrote, "is the true new frontier, not just of science but of humankind itself, and it is my profound hope that what happened to me will bring the world one step closer to accepting it."

Tales like these are thrilling in part because their tellers hold the passionate conviction of religious converts: I saw it, so it must be true. According to a Gallup poll, about 8 million Americans claim to have had a near-death experience (NDE), and many of them regard this experience as proof of an afterlife—a parallel, spiritual realm, more real, many say, than this one. Raymond Moody, who wrote *Life After Life* in 1975, one of the

THE MOUTHS OF BABES

Eleven-year-old Colton Burpo and his father, Todd, sign books about the boy's encounter with heaven at age 3 during surgery.

first popular books about NDEs, told CNN in 2013 that among people who have had such experiences, conviction about an afterlife transcends the particulars of religion. "A lot of people talk about encountering a being of light," he said. "Christians call it Christ. Jewish people say it's an angel. I've gone to different continents, and you can hear the same thing in China, India and Japan about meeting a being of complete love and compassion." Moody was one of the founders of the International Association for Near-Death Studies, a group devoted to building global understanding of such experiences.

It's an inversion, almost, of the old philosophical puzzle: If a tree falls in the forest and there's no one there to hear it, does it make a sound? If you are certain that you saw something (or felt something or heard something), does it mean that it's empirically proven? And if you are predisposed to want to see something, are you likelier to see it, the way Harry Potter saw his dear departed mother in Hogwarts's magic mirror? And finally, if you see something while you are stressed or unconscious or traumatized in some way, does that circumstance delegitimize the veracity of your vision? This is the trouble with NDEs as a field of scientific study: you can't have a control group. Most people on the brink of dying do die (and so cannot describe what that process is like), and those who survive approach the brink in such different ways—car accident, stroke, heart attack—that it's impossible to compare their experiences empirically. But over the years, science has posited a number of

THE FACTS OF FAITH
Neuroscientist Andrew Newberg, who has applied clinical methods to the study of the relationship between spirituality and the mind, says some aspects of NDEs can be explained scientifically (but not definitively).

theories about the connection between visions of heaven and the chemical and physical processes that occur at death.

Andrew Newberg is a neuroscientist and professor at Thomas Jefferson University and Hospital and has made his reputation studying the brain scans of religious people (nuns and monks) who have ecstatic experiences as they meditate. He believes the "tunnel" and the "light" that NDE-ers so frequently describe can be easily explained. As your eyesight fades, you lose the peripheral areas first, he points out. "That's why you'd have a tunnel sensation." If you see a bright light, that could be the central part of the visual system shutting down last.

Newberg puts forward the following scenario, which he emphasizes is guesswork: When people die, two parts of the brain that usually work in opposition to each other act cooperatively. The sympathetic nervous system—a web of nerves and neurons that run through the spinal cord and spread to virtually every organ in the body—is responsible for arousal or excitement. It gets you ready for action. The parasympathetic system, with which the sympathetic system is entwined, calms you down and rejuvenates you. In life, the turning on of one system promotes the shutting down of the other. The sympathetic nervous system kicks in when a car cuts you off on the highway; the parasympathetic system is in charge as you're falling asleep. But in the brains of people having mystical experiences, and perhaps in death, both systems are fully "on," giving a person a sensation both of slowing down, being "out of body," and of seeing things vividly, including memories of important people and past events. It is possible, Newberg asserts—though not at all certain—that visions of heaven are merely chemical and neurological events that occur during death.

Since at least the 1980s, scientists have theorized that NDEs occur as a kind of physiological defense mechanism. In order to guard against damage during trauma, the brain releases protective chemicals that also happen to trigger intense hallucinations. This theory gained traction after scientists realized that virtually all of the features of an NDE—a sense of moving through a tunnel, an out-of-body feeling, spiritual awe, visual hallucinations, intense memories—can be reproduced with a stiff dose of ketamine, a horse tranquilizer frequently used as a party drug. In 2000 a psychiatrist named Karl Jansen wrote a book called *Ketamine: Dreams and Realities*, in which he interviewed a number of recreational users. One of them described a drug trip in a way that might be familiar to Dante, or the author of Revelation. "I came out into a golden Light. I rose into the Light and found myself having an unspoken exchange with the Light, which I believed to be God ... I didn't believe in God, which made the experience even more startling.

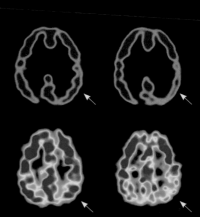

This is your brain on spirituality

In Newberg's brain scans of Tibetan Buddhists (top) and Franciscan nuns (bottom), the lower right side of the brain shows up as yellow during meditation or prayer, rather than the red seen on the left-hand "baseline" images, indicating decreased activity in the area responsible for our sense of orientation in space and time.

Afterwards, I walked around the house for hours saying 'Mine eyes have seen the glory of the coming of the Lord.' "

For some scientists, however, purely scientific explanations of heavenly visions do not suffice. Emily Williams Kelly is a psychologist who works at the University of Virginia's Division of Perceptual Studies, which treats the study of NDEs as legitimate science. Her résumé is impressive: she has degrees from Duke, the University of Virginia and the University of Edinburgh—not institutions one usually associates with the study of the supernatural or paranormal. Kelly has spent her career researching, as she puts it, "the interface between the brain and the mind." Practically speaking, she interviews dying people and tries to find patterns among their similarities. Kelly believes the experiences of people who have had near-death visions demonstrate that consciousness exists even after normal brain function ceases. (She would seem to provide some corroboration for Eben Alexander's claims.) This theory, she argues, could suggest explanations for the afterlife: "If our conscious experience totally depends on the brain, then there can't be an afterlife—when the brain is gone, the mind is gone. But it's not that simple. Even when the brain seems to be virtually disabled, people are still having these experiences."

What is she saying? That upon death, people really go to another realm? And that science can prove it? Kelly shrugs. NDEs "tell us to open our minds and think there may be a great deal more to mind and consciousness—that's as far as I'm willing to go."

When Alexander published his book in 2012, drawing on the work of Kelly and her husband, Edward, he drew derision, as he knew he would, from broad segments of the rationalist and scientific communities. Having fallen into a coma after contracting bacterial meningitis, he saw incredible things. "I was a speck on a beautiful butterfly wing," he said in an interview, "millions of other butterflies around us. We were flying through blooming flowers, blossoms on trees, and they were all coming out as we flew through them … [There were] waterfalls, pools of water, indescribable colors, and above there were these arcs of silver and gold light and beautiful hymns coming down from them. Indescribably gorgeous hymns. I later came to call them 'angels,' those arcs of light in the sky." This experience convinced him beyond any doubt of the existence of a loving God and the ability of souls to travel to the realms where God lives. The idea of a godless universe "now lies broken at our feet," he wrote in his book. "What happened to me destroyed it, and I intend to spend the rest of my life investigating the true nature of consciousness and making the fact that we are more, much more than our physical brains as clear as I can."

MODERN SKEPTICISM
Neuroscientist and author Sam Harris criticized Alexander's retelling of his heavenly experience, calling it an "archaeological artifact that is certain to embarrass us in the eyes of future generations."

The rationalist author Sam Harris, who is also a neuroscientist, aimed a fierce critique at Alexander's account of his NDE. On his blog, Harris wrote that while he had no particular convictions about the essence or origins of consciousness, he was quite sure Alexander's argument was specious. No one's cerebral cortex shuts down entirely during coma, Harris pointed out. Additionally, the doctor showed no understanding of the kinds of neurotransmitters that can be released by the brain during trauma, including one called DMT, which produces hallucinations. "Let me suggest that, whether or not heaven exists, Alexander sounds precisely how a scientist should not sound when he doesn't know what he is talking about," Harris concluded.

MEDICAL MIRACLE
Eben Alexander, a neurosurgeon who has operated on thousands of brains in his career, had an NDE while in a coma and believes science can establish the reality of heaven.

My own concern is somewhat different, relating back to the tree-in-the-forest conundrum. I believe Alexander (and all the others who testify to having visited heaven) saw what he says he saw, but one person's vision, seen during trauma, does not add up to proof. Further, all the emphasis on Alexander's scientific credentials that accompanied the marketing of his book is disingenuous and entirely beside the point: the veracity of a vision of heaven would have nothing to do with where one went to medical school.

7

on earth as it is in heaven

The Holy Monastery of Rousanou in Greece, with its skyward-reaching rock formations, evokes a secluded earthly paradise.

St. Joseph's Abbey is built on a hilltop in central Massachusetts with ranging views of New England woods and farmlands, and on the summer day I visited several years ago, it looked very much—explicitly— like heaven.

High stone walls encircle the monastery buildings, which seemed to grow organically from the ground. Pathways crisscross lawns and commons, and everywhere fruit trees bloomed. The monks who live there wear sandals and belted white cassocks, giving them the appearance of the angels you see in popular cartoons, and when I gazed through a window into a sunny room, I saw one of them playing a harp. As Trappists, these men have taken vows of silence. The only sound they make with their voices is the singing they do, seven times a day, when they chant the psalms in a ritual called the Divine Office.

In medieval times, monasteries were built to resemble, literally, heaven on earth. They were cloistered, separate, of this world but outside it. Their residents abided close to God and busied themselves with godly occupations: song, prayer, care for the poor, teaching, learning, and meditating on God's word. Even today, monks regard their radical withdrawal from the world as a kind of living martyrdom, an emulation of the activities of heaven. "Mortality," one of the brothers at St. Joseph's told me (after having been given permission by his abbot to speak), "is not abstract here."

Even before Jesus died and, according to Scripture, rose again, people were creating heavenly societies on earth. The Essenes, the Jewish sect that inhabited the desert in what is now Israel, lived an ascetic, communal life. When they prayed together, they believed, they were not just appealing to God or singing his praises; they were mirroring in real time the activities of angels in heaven.

And when Jesus died and the world did not end, his followers were faced with a choice, of sorts—one that divides believers even

QUIET BLISS
A monk walks in the Great Cloister of St. Joseph's Abbey in Spencer, Mass., where Trappists silently roam verdant pathways that emulate a tranquil, heavenly setting.

DESERT SANCTUARY
In 1947 a boy discovered the manuscripts known as the Dead Sea Scrolls in a cave at the site of Qumran, which was an ancient center of the ascetic Jewish community the Essenes.

today. Do you believe that heaven, translated in Jewish scripture as *olam ha-ba*, the world to come, is a prize for the righteous at the end of time? Or do you believe that heaven is attainable, in glimmers, right now, when humans endeavor to do God's work on earth?

Monasticism has long been a way for Christians to live out an idea of heaven on earth by way of solitude—like Saint Anthony, who in the third century shut himself in a cave with very little food or water for, as legend has it, 20 years, and emerged younger and more vital than before: exactly like an angel, onlookers said. "His soul was free from blemish," wrote Anthony's biographer Athanasius, "for it was neither contracted as if by grief, nor relaxed by pleasure nor possessed by laughter or dejection." In his cave, Anthony learned to embody the promise of Revelation, which is that in heaven God "shall wipe away every tear." In the Middle Ages, visions of heaven on earth became grand and opulent, the result of a powerful church in a feudal time: the spires of cathedrals scraped the sky. In the first universities, men on earth learned to pore over the word of God. Even today, orthodox Jews joke that the Jewish idea of heaven is like school. "It's Torah study," one scholar quipped to me, "without recess."

America was founded, after the Protestant Reformation, by groups of Christians seeking to implement in one way or another their own idiosyncratic ideas of the perfections of heaven. These were communal societies, inspired by the accounts of the first-century church in Acts 4: "Now the whole group of those who believed were of one heart and soul, and no one claimed private ownership of any possessions, but everything they owned was held in common." The Puritans, of course, kept their minds constantly on the rewards of heaven, and they saw themselves as exemplary models of Christian life, devotion and piety. When John Winthrop, one of the first governors of Massachusetts, said, "We shall be as a city upon a hill," he was

LIFE OF LEARNING
A monk in the Cistercian Wettingen-Mehrerau Abbey in Austria. In many traditions, studying the word of God has been a vital part of earthly preparation for heaven.

BOUNTY IN SIMPLICITY
Horse-drawn buggies on a road in Pennsylvania. The Amish believe their communities, segregated from the pressures of modernity, will help them lead a saintly way of life.

ONE WITH NATURE
A practitioner of Wicca finds spirituality in a forest in Switzerland. Wiccans see hints of the hereafter in elements of the natural world.

comparing his colonial outpost to heaven—the New Jerusalem.

More individualistic conceptions of heaven on earth flourished here as well. The Amish rejected modernity to live as much as possible like a community of saints in the world (in a Protestant reference to the ascetic communities of early Christianity). The Ephrata Cloister, established in the Pennsylvania wilderness in 1732, was named after what the biblical Hebrews called Jerusalem. Its members would wake for two hours in the middle of each night to await the arrival of Christ. Shakers, so called because when possessed by the Holy Spirit they trembled violently, established communities in the late 18th and early 19th centuries. They made wooden furniture so exquisite that the American monk Thomas Merton wrote in 1966 that "the peculiar grace of a Shaker chair is due to the fact that it was made by someone capable of believing that an angel might come and sit on it."

In modern times, it can be said that heaven is visible all the time, if only in glimmers. Its appearance, how it feels, depends largely on who's looking. Heaven is accessible through psychics and channelers to those who wish to talk with their lost loved ones. Pay a fee and gain access to the inhabitants of another realm. It's palpable to leftist believers who devote themselves to justice: "The only thing we can do about people," said the Catholic reformer Dorothy Day, "is to love them." Some people find heaven in music, and not only in Bach; the writer Rick Moody imagines that in heaven he will hear whatever music he wants whenever he wants to hear it, even when he yearns for the sound of a band like Rush. For the growing numbers of adherents to earth's religions—paganism, Wicca and

SONGS OF THE HEART

A choir presents a gospel concert in Paris. For many believers, heaven is evoked by the music that moves us here on earth.

so on—an afterlife is evidenced in nature: in the riffling of leaves and the setting sun and the way the light sparkles on the ocean in daylight. (For more conventional believers, these images are powerful evidence, too, of another world. *Almost Heaven*, a painting by Thomas Kinkade, shows a man fishing in a glacial lake someplace like Montana.) Diane Keaton made a strange little movie called *Heaven* in 1987, and in it a couple laughingly say they thought heaven might be something like sex.

Mimi the ape did not want the orphan Lipopo to be lost forever; she railed fiercely against the cold, hard fact of death. Humans through history have tried more sophisticated ways—language and paint and music and reason and science—to explain or mute the inevitable pain, but in the end the problem is the same. We do not want our love to end. Human love, between friends and spouses and especially between parents and children, is often cited in sermons as the best metaphor for God's enduring and supernatural love for humankind. And if that is true, if God is love and heaven is where God lives, then the love between people—and the striving to be kind in spite of our impulses toward selfishness—is where heaven can sometimes be found even amid the busy, anxious chores of life. At least that's true for me. When I snuggle my child at bedtime or, in the quiet early-morning dark, inch closer to my husband, I sometimes try to make time stand still. If I'm quiet enough, in the overpowering love between and among us, I can sometimes feel what it might be like in heaven—a place of overwhelming, eternal joy and love, beyond the reach of a skeptic's doubts.

"Heaven is under our feet as well as over our heads."

—Henry David Thoreau

CREDITS

TITLE PAGE 1 *Jacob's Ladder* by Avignon School, Musée du Petit Palais Avignon, photo by Gianni Dagli Orti/The Art Archive at Art Resource, NY **CONTENTS 2** Sung-Il Kim/Corbis **INTRODUCTION 4** *The Dream of Jacob* by Marc Chagall, Musée National Marc Chagall, Nice, France, photo by Gérard Blot RMN-Grand Palais/Art Resource, NY, © 2014 Artists Rights Society (ARS), NY/ADAGP, Paris **CHAPTER 1 8** Elysian Fields (detail) 3rd-c. fresco, Museo Nazionale Romano, Rome, photo by Alfredo Dagli Orti/The Art Archive at Art Resource, NY **11** Book of the Dead of Heruben (detail) Egyptian 21st-dynasty papyrus, Egyptian National Museum, Cairo/photo by BEBA/AISA/Bridgeman Art Library **12** Eyal Warshavsky/Corbis **13** Mahmoud Illean/Demotix/Corbis **14** Corey Weiner/Alamy **17** *The Prophet Elijah in the Wilderness and His Fiery Ascent into Heaven*, c. 1600, Russian School/Mark Gallery, London, UK/The Bridgeman Art Library **18** Indranil Mukherjee/AFP/Getty Images **20** *The Death of Socrates*, 1787, Catharine Lorillard Wolfe Collection, Wolfe Fund, 1931 (31.45), The Metropolitan Museum of Art, NY, photo © The Metropolitan Museum of Art/Art Resource, NY **22** (clockwise from top left) *Disputation over the Most Holy Sacrament* by Raphael, Vatican/Corbis; *Hope, Reaching for Heaven, Stands Among Sad and Happy Men, Joys, and Fear*, c. 1512/1515, pen and brown ink on laid paper/National Gallery of Art, Washington D.C.; *The Peaceable Kingdom* by Edward Hicks, c. 1840-1845, Brooklyn Museum/Corbis; *Jacob's Ladder* by William Blake, 18th c./The Gallery Collection/Corbis **23** (from top) Paramount Pictures/The Everett Collection; *Book with Wings* by Anselm Kiefer, lead, tin and steel, 1992-94/Modern Art Museum of Fort Worth; Comedy Central/Everett Collection **CHAPTER 2 24** *Paradise and Ascension into the Empyrean* (detail) by Hieronymus Bosch, Palazzo Ducale, Venice, photo by Cameraphoto Arte/Art Resource, NY **27** Godong/UIG/Getty Images **28** *Ascent of the Prophet Muhammad to Heaven* by Aqa Mirak, Persian; British Library, London, UK, © British Library Board/Bridgeman Art Library **31** The Ebstorf World Map of 1284, by Gervasius of Tilbury, facsimile (original destroyed in 1945 in Hanover) **32** Wood engraving (colorized) by unknown artist, Mary Evans Picture Library/Science Source **34** *The Last Judgment*, detail of the resurrection of the dead, c. 1445-50 by Rogier van der Weyden, Hotel Dieu, Beaune, France/Bridgeman Art Library **36** *The City of God*, from a translation of the works of Saint Augustine by Raoul de Presles, c. 1469-73 (vellum) by French School, Bibliotheque Nationale, Paris, Archives Charmet/Bridgeman Art Library **39** Illustration from *The Desert of Religion, and Other Poems and Religious Pieces*, originally published in England, 1st half of 15th century, photo © British Library Board/Robana/Art Resource, NY **40** Raghu Rai/Magnum Photos **42** Andrew Holbrooke/Corbis **43** Pope selling indulgences (detail), woodcut from *Passional Christi und Anti Christi*, 1521, J. Rhau Grunenberg Wittenberg, The Pierpont Morgan Library, NY, photo by The Pierpont Morgan Library/Art Resource, NY **CHAPTER 3 44** *The Church Militant and Triumphant* (detail of Saint Peter at the gate to heaven) by Andrea di Bonaiuto, c. 1368, fresco, Spanish Chapel, S. Maria Novella, Florence, Italy, photo by Scala/Art Resource, NY **47** *Saint Bernard preaching the Second Crusades* from the 15th-c. manuscript *Les passages d'Outre-Mer*, Bibliotheque Nationale, Paris, photo by Snark/Art Resource, NY **48** Charles Ommanney/Getty Images **50** Courtesy of The Church of Jesus Christ of Latter-Day Saints **51** Michael Robinson-Chavez/The Washington Post/Getty Images **52** Jim Lo Scalzo/EPA/Corbis **54** Mindy Schauer/The Orange County Register/Zuma Press **55** Graphic by TIME **CHAPTER 4 57** Illustration from *The Divine Comedy* by Dante Alighieri, 1885 (digitally colored engraving) by Gustave Doré (after), private collection, photo by Costa/Leemage/Bridgeman Art Library **59** Triumphal arch: *The Heavenly Jerusalem* (detail), Early Christian mosaic, 5th c., S. Maria Maggiore, Rome, photo by Nimatallah/Art Resource, NY **60** (from top) *Christ Enthroned with the Apostles in the Heavenly Jerusalem* (detail) Apse mosaic, early Christian, 410–417, S. Pudenziana, Rome, photo by Scala/Art Resource, NY; *Garden of Paradise*, c. 1415, by Master of Oberrheinischer, Stadelsches Kunstinstitut, Frankfurt-am-Main, Germany/Bridgeman Art Library; *La Primavera*, c. 1482, by Sandro Botticelli, photo by Universal History Archive/Getty Images **62** The Angels in Paradise, detail from *The Last Judgment* by Fra Angelico, fresco (c. 1436), Museo di S. Marco, Florence, photo by Erich Lessing/Art Resource, NY **65** Damian Dovarganes/AP Images **66** *Dante and His Poem* by Domenico di Michelino, c. 1465, Duomo, Florence, Italy, photo by Scala/Art Resource, NY **68** *The Pilgrim's Progress, or, Christian's Journey from the City of Destruction in This Evil World to the Celestial City in the World That Is to Come*, copperplate map with added color, 1813, Historic Maps Collection/Princeton University Library **69** *Girls of Ann Smith Academy Visiting Stonewall Jackson's Grave, Lexington* by Michael Miley, 1866, glass-plate negative, Accession No. 1940.20.344.A-B, Miley Collection/Virginia Historical Society **70** Geffen Pictures/courtesy Photofest **71** Paramount/courtesy Everett Collection **CHAPTER 5 75** *Buddha Descending from Heaven* (wall painting) by Thai School, 18th c., National Museum, Bangkok, Thailand, photo by Luca Tettoni/Bridgeman Art Library **77** *Dharmachakra, Wheel of Transmigratory Existence* (paper) by Tibetan School; American Museum of Natural History, NY, photo by Boltin Picture Library/Bridgeman Art Library **78** Paul Saltzman/Contact Press Images **79** Allyse Pulliam/Demotix/Corbis **80** Xinhua/Eyevine/Redux **81** Stefano De Luigi/VII/Corbis **82** Gerald Martineau/The Washington Post/Getty Images **85** Hungry Ghost scroll, late 12th c., Kyoto National Museum, Kyoto, Japan **86** Menahem Kahana/AFP/Getty Images **CHAPTER 6 88** George Diebold/Getty Images **91** Andrei Malov/Dreamstime.com (manipulated photo) **92** Courtesy of Don Piper Ministries **93** Fred Hunt/The New York Times/Redux **94** Matt Rourke/AP Images **95** Courtesy of Dr. Andrew Newberg **96** Deborah Feingold/Corbis Outline **97** Photo by Jurvetson/Flickr **CHAPTER 7 98** Michael Falzone/JAI/Corbis **101** Courtesy of St. Joseph's Abbey, Spencer, MA **102** Hans P. Szyszka/NA/Novarc/Corbis **104** Toni Anzenberger/Redux **106** Education Images/UIG/Getty Images **108** Elleringmann/LAIF/Redux **109** Philippe Lissac/Godong/Corbis **110** Creative Travel Projects/Shutterstock

FRONT COVER (top to bottom) Jacob's ladder by Cypriot (detail), fresco, Kykkos Monastery, Troodos Mountains, Cyprus/Bridgeman Art Library; *The Last Judgment* by Jan Provost II (detail), oil on panel, Hamburger Kunsthalle, Hamburg, Germany/Bridgeman Art Library; illustration from *The Divine Comedy* (detail) by Dante Alighieri, 1885 (digitally enhanced image), illustration from *The Doré Gallery*, published c. 1890 by Gustave Doré, private collection/Bridgeman Art Library; *The Angels in Planet Mercury* (detail) (digitally enhanced image), illustration from *The Doré Gallery*, published c. 1890 by Gustave Doré, private collection/Bridgeman Art Library; *The Gods of Olympus* (detail) by Giulio Romano (workshop of), trompe l'oeil ceiling (fresco) from the Sala dei Giganti, 1528, Palazzo del Te, Mantua, Italy/Bridgeman Art Library; *Last Judgment* (detail) by Giorgio-Giulio Clovio (circle of), after Michelangelo, c. 1570 (parchment), Casa Buonarroti, Florence, Italy/Bridgeman Art Library; The New Jerusalem (detail), number 80 from *The Apocalypse of Angers*, 1373–87 (tapestry) by Nicolas Bataille, Musée des Tapisseries, Angers, France/Bridgeman Art Library; *Last Judgment* (detail), copy of version by Fra Angelico in Berlin Museum with Pope Pius V added, from church of the convent of Bosco Marengo, Galleria Sabauda Turin, photo by Gianni Dagli Orti/The Art Archive at Art Resource, NY **BACK COVER** *The Angels in the Planet Mercury: Beatrice Ascends with Dante to the Planet Mercury*, c. 1860-68 (engraving) by Gustave Doré (after), private collection/Bridgeman Art Library

TIME

Managing Editor Nancy Gibbs
Design Director D.W. Pine
Director of Photography Kira Pollack

VISIONS OF HEAVEN

Writer Lisa Miller
Editor Damon Linker
Designer Skye Gurney
Photo Editor Patricia Cadley
Reporter Andréa Ford
Editorial Production David Sloan

Time Home Entertainment

Publisher Jim Childs
Vice President, Brand & Digital Strategy Steven Sandonato
Executive Director, Marketing Services Carol Pittard
Executive Director, Retail & Special Sales Tom Mifsud
Executive Publishing Director Joy Butts
Director, Bookazine Development & Marketing Laura Adam
Vice President, Finance Vandana Patel
Publishing Director Megan Pearlman
Associate General Counsel Helen Wan
Assistant Director, Special Sales Ilene Schreider
Brand Manager Bryan Christian
Associate Production Manager Kimberly Marshall
Associate Prepress Manager Alex Voznesenskiy

Editorial Director Stephen Koepp
Senior Editor Roe D'Angelo
Copy Chief Rina Bander
Design Manager Anne-Michelle Gallero
Editorial Operations Gina Scauzillo
Special Thanks Don Armstrong, Katherine Barnet, Jeremy Biloon, Eliza Castro, Susan Chodakiewicz, Rose Cirrincione, Christine Font, Diane Francis, Hillary Hirsch, David Kahn, Amy Mangus, Nina Mistry, Dave Rozzelle, Ricardo Santiago, Adriana Tierno, Time Inc. Premedia, TIME Research Center

Parts of this book were adapted from *Heaven: Our Enduring Fascination with the Afterlife*, by Lisa Miller (HarperCollins, 2010).